Ulrich Schliewen

Aquarium Fish

How to Care for Them,
Feed Them, and
Understand Them

With photographs by expert aquarium photographers
Illustrations: Renate Holzner

BARRON'S

CONTENTS

3 Understand, learn, and observe

A General Importance

Children's Corner

Learn facts about fish before buying

From A to Z, successful care of ornamental fish depends upon knowledge about their ecology.

What You Should Know About Fish

Most aquarium fish are captured in the wild or are the offspring of fish that were captured in the wild. It is not possible for an aquarium to be a true reproduction of the natural world. However, if you understand the ecology of the fish that you would like to keep, you will be able to successfully care for them in an aquarium environment.

Every Fish Species Has Special Requirements

Nature has created more than 25,000 fish species. Each individual species has adapted, over geological time, to its own special environment.

The habitats of most aquarium fish are the tropical regions of South and Central America, Africa, Asia, and Australia. Water conditions favored by individual species can vary widely, however. For instance, some species come from streams with a fast current and very hard water, whereas others come from still, very soft waters.

Many of the best-known aquarium fish come from blackwater streams.

An Asiatic fish species, the five-banded barb (*Barbus pentazona*) is at home in blackwater streams.

Fish Are Sensitive Creatures

If the habitat requirements of the different fish species are met, they thrive. If not, they waste away and finally die.

Of course there are robust species that can tolerate a wide range of maintenance conditions, but even these possess delicate senses with which they perceive their surroundings and check whether conditions are suitable. Delicate species make use of the same fine sensibility but have special requirements. The robust species as well as the delicate ones are suitable for keeping in an aquarium, if you fulfill their requirements with the appropriate maintenance.

Thus, to enjoy healthy fish in your aquarium, it is impor-

9

tant to become knowledgeable about their special requirements before you buy them. Then you can provide them with the living conditions they need to thrive.

The tables in the profile section of this book, beginning on page 14, give you important information about the maintenance requirements of many species.

Wild-caught or Captive-bred?

The question of whether you should get fish captured in the wild or captive-bred does not have a clear-cut answer, for there are qualitative differences between them.

Wild-caught, that is, fish taken directly from the wild, demand more care than captive-bred fish of the same species. They have already lived part of their life under natural conditions and have adapted to them. Thus, wild fish often display more beautiful colors, and—under optimal conditions—are more robust than those that have been captive-bred. But this only applies if the capture and transport have been properly carried out and the fish have been carefully acclimated by the wholesaler.

TIP

Take a good tropical fish book with you to the tropical fish dealer. Check the required care conditions described for a particular fish species against the possibilities that you can offer in your aquarium at home. This way, you will avoid any possible disappointments at the beginning.

Apple snails are popular inhabitants for community aquariums.

How Long Do Fish Live?

There are fish that can live longer than twenty years. Others don't even live for one year. Fish with a short life span often come from marshes that dry out for part of the year. Before they die, they must provide for offspring. They lay their eggs in the soil. These remain there until the next rain. When the marsh fills with water again, the young hatch from the eggs. They grow so fast that they reproduce in the same year. However, the famous lungfishes, which also live in such marshes, can become very old. During the dry spells, they burrow into the soil to wait for the next rain.

Captive-bred fish have usually adapted to aquarium conditions over many generations and therefore are often easier to care for. They are not necessarily inferior in appearance to the wild-caught fish if they have been raised from good breeding stock.

Because you can't always know the origins or the import history there is only one thing to do: Use the photographs and details in this book to check whether the fish appear healthy and whether they are behaving normally.

Chose the more robust-looking individuals, whether the fish are wild-caught or captive-bred.

Environmental Protection and the Aquarium

Anyone who has observed the wonderful life in an aquarium knows how important it is to preserve and protect the natural world.

There have been many conservation initiatives developed to preserve the tropical environment from which most wild-caught aquarium fish come. The environments are maintained with the help of funds that come from capturing tropical fish. The people who catch and sell tropical fish in a particular place also have an interest in keeping the natural regions intact. Otherwise their most important source of earnings would be irretrievably lost.

Legal Issues Related to Aquarium Keeping

Lease Law

Individuals contemplating the installation of an aquarium in their home or apartment should take a moment to reflect on legal issues that may arise. Aquariums are different from other home furnishings, largely because they are rather heavy, about 10 lb (4.5 kg) per gal (3.8 L) of tank capacity. (Water itself weighs 8.5 lb (4 kg) per gal (3.8 L), and the tank and its equipment account for the additional weight.) Further, because transparency is required, the materials used for constructing aquarium tanks, that is, glass and acrylic plastic, are subject to breakage. These two properties of aquariums can lead to all sorts of dire scenarios in the minds of lawyers, insurance adjusters, and landlords. Thus, it is to your advantage to do some research before installing an aquarium in your residence. The issues involved become more significant as the tank becomes larger. A 10-gal (38-L) aquarium on the kitchen counter might make a mess if broken; a 200-gal (757-L) system crashing through the floor into the apartment below can fatally injure a person. Common sense, above all, must prevail in regard to the installation of your aquarium system.

If you live in an apartment or rental house, you may require permission from your landlord for an aquarium, and you may have to comply with the landlord's wishes regarding the size of the system you can install. Check your lease. Also, determine the load-bearing capacity of the floor, especially if you live above ground level. Check with the landlord, building superintendent, or a contractor.

Insurance Law

If you own your home, you won't need anyone's permission, but the situation may be more complex. Your aquarium installation may need to comply with local building codes; check with a contractor or the codes enforcement office responsible for your location. Residential floors often have load-bearing capacities of 100 lb (45 kg) per sq ft (sq m). This would translate into an aquarium of about 40 gal (151 L). A larger tank would require reinforcements to the underlying structure. You may need a special endorsement on your homowner's insurance policy to cover damage or injuries if the tank should break, leak, or fall through the floor. Check with your insurance agent.

Building codes, insurance regulations, landlord-tenant laws, and laws governing liabilities in case of accidents all vary from state to state. If you are unsure about your rights or responsibilities, you should seek legal counsel before commencing the installation of the aquarium. This is especially true for a large, complex, or costly system—anything larger than about 100 gal (379 L). Fortunately, most tanks never leak. Aquarium accidents are uncommon, but they do happen. It is only prudent to take all precautions against the possibility.

Sales Contract Law

Another set of legal issues has to do with your relationship to the dealer from whom you buy aquarium equipment, supplies, and, especially, fish and other living organisms. Generally speaking, aquarium products are covered by warranties similiar to those covering most other consumer goods, and a truly defective product can be returned or exchanged without a problem.

Live organisms are another matter, and policies vary from store to store. The best approach is to assume that once you leave the store with a fish or other live purchase, the store will assume no further responsibility for the behavior, health, or survival of that specimen. This is why it is important for the hobbyist to understand the requirements of any specimen before it is purchased, to learn to recognize the signs of poor health that may be evident in the dealer's tank, and to quarantine new acquisitions for awhile in a separate tank before introducing them into an established aquarium.

In particular, educate yourself about the disposition and ultimate size of any species you are considering. Few dealers are willing to accept returns of specimens that have outgrown their quarters or become too aggressive toward their tankmates, as the market for such specimens is obviously a small one.

Animal Protection

Even tropical fish in the biotope aquarium must be kept in the manner appropriate to their species and behavior patterns. This means not only a diet that is appropriate but also the right environmental conditions in the aquarium. Regular water changes are part of this, as are suitable aquarium decorations.

Sometimes, it is even important for fish to have the correct social milieu in order to thrive. Many small tetras, for example, if kept individually will assume faded colors and hide among the aquarium decorations. Keeping these same fish under more natural conditions, that is, in a shoal of five to seven individuals, results in their spending time in the open, displaying their brilliant coloration.

Bala or silver sharks (*Balantiocheilus melanopterus*); see page 115.

The Most Popular Aquarium Fish

The following profile section introduces by groups more than 120 of the most popular fish. The introduction to each fish group gives information about the group's distribution, lifestyle, special features, and generally applicable maintenance requirements. The tables give important information for the proper care of individual species.

Explanation of the Tables

English name: The most common name is given, if any.

Latin name: It consists of the genus name followed by the species name.

Size: Attainable maximum size for the species.

Tank: Minimum possible tank size that should be used to permit the species to develop its typical behavior patterns. For special purposes, for example, breeding or the care of single animals, you can also choose smaller tanks.

Water type: Divided into six types. Most of the fish described can be kept in different types of water. Therefore, more than one water type is often noted for any one species.

The particular water types have the following chemical characteristics (see page 58):

■ Type 1: pH 4.5–6.5; degrees dKH: 0–3 (soft)
■ Type 2: pH 5.5–6.8; degrees dKH: 3–8 (average)
■ Type 3: pH 6.8–7.5; degrees dKH: 3–8 (average)
■ Type 4: pH 7.5–8.5; degrees dKH: 8–16 (hard)
■ Type 5: pH 7.2–8.0; degrees dKH: > 12 (hard)
■ Type 6: pH > 8.0; degrees dKH: > 12 (hard)

Photo: Refers to the photograph of the particular species in the book.

Black widows
(***Gymnocorymbus ternetzi***).

**Top: Neon tetras
(*Paracheirodon innesi*).**

**Bottom: Emperor tetra male
(*Nematobrycon palmeri*).**

Characins

The fish of this group are among the most popular aquarium fish because they bring magnificent color to the aquarium. The shining neon tetras of the dark jungle streams of the Amazon rain forest are typical characins.

Distinguishing marks: Most characins differ from other similar-looking aquarium fish like barbs and live-bearing fish by an additional fin, the so-called adipose fin. It lies between the dorsal and caudal fins. This characteristic may not be definitive, however, because there are also characin species that do not have an adipose fin.

Habits in the wild: The characins shown here are mostly found in clear streams and quiet river sections in tropical South America. Only the Congo tetras come from Africa. The native waters of the characins are often covered with water plants. The fallen branches and leaves of the ancient forest trees growing on the banks structure their surroundings. The characins swim in small groups, or schools, to search for small food animals in open water around them. The schools are always ready to rush quickly for the open water if any imaginable danger threatens them. Smaller characin species, especially, also seek the smallest plant and animal food particles at the roots of the water plants or in the tangle of leaves that cover the water surface.

15

Characins

Fish Species	Size	Tank	Water Type	Temperature	Photo
Congo tetra *Phenacogrammus interruptus*	5 in (13 cm)	39 in (100 cm)	2–5	73–81°F (23–27°C)	page 17 top
Cardinal tetra *Paracheirodon axelrodi*	2 in (5 cm)	24 in (60 cm)	1–3	73–81°F (23–27°C)	pages 102–103
Neon tetra *Paracheirodon innesi*	1½ in (4 cm)	20 in (50 cm)	1–5	68–75°F (20–24°C)	page 15 top
Emperor tetra *Nematobrycon palmeri*	2½ in (6 cm)	24 in (60 cm)	2–5	73–79°F (23–26°C)	page 15 bottom
Marbled hatchetfish *Carnegiella strigata*	2 in (5 cm)	24 in (60 cm)	1–5	79–86°F (26–30°C)	
Black widow *Gymnocorymbus ternetzi*	2½ in (6 cm)	24 in (60 cm)	2–6	73–82°F (23–28°C)	page 14
Red-nose tetra *Hemigrammus bleheri*	2 in (5 cm)	24 in (60 cm)	1–3	72–79°F (22–26°C)	
Bleeding heart tetra *Hemigrammus erythozonus*	1½ in (4 cm)	20 in (50 cm)	1–5	73–79°F (23–26°C)	pages 80–81
Black wedge tetra *Hemigrammus pulcher*	1¾ in (4.5 cm)	24 in (60 cm)	1–3	75–82°F (24–28°C)	page 18 bottom
Jewel tetra *Hyphessobrycon callistus*	1¾ in (4.5 cm)	24 in (60 cm)	1–5	75–82°F (24–28°C)	page 17 bottom
Rosey-finned tetra *Hyphessobrycon rosaceus*	2 in (5 cm)	24 in (60 cm)	2–5	73–81°F (23–27°C)	
Phantom tetra *Megalomphodus megalopterus*	1¾ in (4.5 cm)	24 in (60 cm)	2–5	73–82°F (23–28°C)	
Diamond tetra *Moenkhausia pittieri*	2½ in (6 cm)	32 in (80 cm)	2–3	75–82°F (24–28°C)	page 64
Red-eyed tetra *Moenkhausia sanctaefilomenae*	2¾ in (7 cm)	32 in (80 cm)	2–6	73–79°F (23°–26°C)	page 18 top
Penguin fish *Thayeria boehlkei*	2½ in (6 cm)	32 in (80 cm)	2–5	75–82°F (24–28°C)	

Only adult Congo tetras (*Phenacogrammus interruptus*) show beautiful coloration.

flooded rain forest floor to avail themselves of the abundant food supply.

Reproduction: Many small eggs are laid on water plants, algae, or fallen leaves. Most characins do not care for their young.

Sexing: Full-grown males of most species are more colorful than the females. The females, on the other hand, are fuller than the males. In fry and in hatchetfish, the sexes are almost impossible to determine.

In the rainy season, when the waters overflow their banks, many characins swarm out onto the now

Like most characins, jewel tetras (*Hyphessobrycon callistus*) love swimming in a school.

Care: Because characins are usually school fish, at least six fish, but even better, ten should be kept together. Because most species like to swim a great deal, I recommend a fairly large tank, even for the smaller species. Water plants next to open swimming areas offer sufficient opportunities to withdraw.

A dark substrate surface allows the often delicate colors of the fish to show up more strongly. Characins do not feel comfortable in a brilliantly lit tank. The males of some species, for example, the emperor tetras, dart sideways out of the school and establish a small territory that they defend against other males. In this territory, they display their fins and splendid colors for passing females.

Diet: All the species named here can be fed with dry food. A regular supplement with plankton (frozen or live) increases their liveliness and the intensity of color. Freshly hatched brine shrimp are a high-value supplementary feed, especially for small species. Hatchetfish enjoy small insects, for example, fruit flies.

Combination: Characins, catfish, and other bottom dwellers, such as the dwarf cichlids, have the same water needs and primarily use the lower tank regions for swimming space.

Top: Red-eyed tetra (*Moenkhausia sanctae-filomenae*).

Bottom: Black wedge tetra (*Hemigrammus pulcher*).

18

Tiger or Sumatra barbs (*Barbus tetrazona*) may nip the fins of other fish if they are not fed enough.

Barbs

As speedy swimmers, barbs add life to the aquarium. Because the habitat requirements of many of the species are relatively undemanding, they are known as "beginner fish," although this doesn't apply to all species.

Distinguishing marks: They are easy to confuse with characins. Barbs lack an adipose fin between the dorsal and caudal fins, however.

Habits in the wild: The barb species that are most often kept in aquariums live in the waters of Southeast Asia, rather like the characins in South America. The robust barbs of the genus *Barbus* (also called *Puntius*) burrow in the ground in small groups in the search for plankton. In the cloudy waters that they often inhabit, the little whiskers at the corners of their mouths help them in finding food. These whiskers contain sense organs that help the fish locate food by "taste" and feel. Danios and rasboras, on the other hand, usually inhabit the middle and upper layers of clear, fastflowing water with a pebbly bottom (zebra danio, white cloud). They also live in the warm blackwater swamps

19

Top: White clouds (*Tanichthys albonubes*).
Bottom: Zebra danios (*Brachydanio rerio*).

and streams of the rain-forested lowlands (*Rasbora, Boraras,* but also *Barbus pentazona*), preferring the root networks of the rain forest trees that border the waters where they can quickly hide from danger.

Reproduction: Barbs do not care for their young but lay many small eggs on plants or fallen leaves, or on the pebbles in flowing water.

Sexing: Adult females are fuller than the males. In juvenile fish, the sexes can hardly be told apart.

Care: As lively school fish, they should be kept with at least six to eight companions; they love having space to swim. The *Barbus pentazona*, harlequin fish, and *Boraras maculata* require high-quality water and plenty of plants for retreating. Although the Sumatra barb comes from similar waters, it is less demanding. Because of their origins, the five species in the table, beside the zebra danio, white cloud, and rosy barb, prefer a dark aquarium.

Diet: Dry food can offer a basis for a healthy diet; however, a regular supplement of plankton (frozen or fresh) increases vitality.

Rasbora hengeli don't grow as large as the ordinary harlequin rasbora (**R. heteromorpha**).

Combination: Bottom-dwelling loaches, algae-eaters, and catfish, as well as dwarf cichlids and labyrinth fish are suitable companions. You should not keep the Sumatra barb with long-finned fish (for example, gouramis), because they tend to nip fins, especially in a crowded tank.

Barbs

Fish Species	Size	Tank	Water Type	Temperature	Photo
Tiger or Sumatra barb *Barbus tetrazona*	2³/4 in (7 cm)	32 in (80 cm)	2–5	73–82°F (23–28°C)	page 19
Rosy barb *Barbus conchonius*	4³/4 in (12 cm)	47 in (120 cm)	2–6	64–72°F (18–22°C)	pages 56–57
Barbus pentazona (Barbs are also called *Puntius*)	1³/4 in (4.5 cm)	24 in (60 cm)	1–3	79–84°F (26–29°C)	page 9
Zebra danio *Brachydanio rerio*	2¹/2 in (6 cm)	32 in (80 cm)	2–6	75–81°F (24–27°C)	page 20 bottom
White cloud *Tanichthys albonubes*	1¹/2 in (4 cm)	24 in (60 cm)	2–6	64–72°F (18–22°C)	page 20 top
Spotted Rasbora *Rasbora muculata*	1 in (2.5 cm)	16 in (40 cm)	1–3	77–84°F (25–29°C)	page 107
Rasbora hengeli	1¹/2 in (4 cm)	20 in (50 cm)	1–3	77–82°F (25–28°C)	page 21 top
Harlequin fish *Rasbora heteromorpha*	1³/4 in (4.5 cm)	24 in (60 cm)	2–5	73–82°F (23–28°C)	

Loaches and Algae-eaters

Distinguishing marks: All species belong to the carp family. But within this group, they form different families, with each family having its own characteristics.

Habits in the wild: All species live on the bottom in flowing waters. There in small groups (*Botia* species, *Acanthophthalmus kuhlii*) they search among the pebbles or between sticks, leaves, and stones for food animals. Dwarf loaches are especially social. The loner red-tailed black shark grazes, mainly on the surfaces of wood and stones, for tiny pieces of food. The algae-eating *Crossocheilus siamensis* and the Chinese algae-eater prefer hard bottoms in strong currents.

Reproduction: To a large extent unknown. No brood care.

Sexing: To a large extent unknown.

Care: Large species need large tanks in which they can be kept in groups, as can the smaller species. So that the subordinate fish are not harassed, each animal should have a hiding place. Keep red-tailed black sharks alone.

Loaches

Fish Species	Size	Tank	Water Type	Temperature	Photo
Clown loach *Botia macracanthus*	10 in (25 cm)	59 in (150 cm)	1–5	77–86°F (25–30°C)	pages 2–3
Dwarf loach *Botia sidthimunki*	26 in (65 cm)	24 in (60 cm)	2–6	79–84°F (26–29°C)	
Coolie loach *Acanthophthalmus kuhlii*	2^1/$_2$ in (6 cm) to 4^3/$_4$ in (12 cm)	24 in (60 cm)	1–5	79–86°F (26–30°C)	page 22 center
Chinese algae-eater *Gyrinocheilus aymonieri*	10 in (25 cm)	47 in (120 cm)	2–6	75–82°F (24–28°C)	page 113
Siamese algae-eater *Crossocheilus siamensis*	6 in (15 cm)	39 in (100 cm)	2–5	75–82°F (24–28°C)	page 22 bottom
Suckermouth algae-eater *Gastromyzon* sp.	2^1/$_2$ in (6 cm)	20 in (50 cm)	2–5	72–75°F (22–24°C)	page 23
Red-tailed black shark *Epalzeorhyncus bicolor*	6 in (15 cm)	39 in (100 cm)	2–6	73–82°F (23–28°C)	page 22 top

Top left: Red-tailed black shark (*Epalzeorhyncus bicolor*).

Center left: Coolie loach (*Acanthohthalmus kuhlii*).

Bottom left: *Crossocheilus siamensis*.

Right: A member of the genus *Gastromyzon*.

Diet: Dry food (such as tablets), as well as smaller or larger live food, depending on the species. Vegetable food for algae-eaters and *Crossocheilus* but not for *Gastromyzon* species.

Combination: Fish of the middle and upper water layers. Avoid territorial cichlids. Keep several *Plecostomus* and *Hypostomus* in a tank by themselves, because other species take away their food and they can thus easily starve to death.

23

Live-Bearing Fish

Distinguishing marks: The species described here belong to the distantly related families of the live-bearing toothed carps and the halfbeaks. Males of both families possess an anal fin that changes to a sex organ, which for the live-bearing toothed carps is called a gonopodium.

Habits in the wild: All species, except for the Southeast-Asian halfbeak, are extremely lively school fish and live in sun-dappled waters in Central America.

There they prefer hard, alkaline water; some species in coastal areas even live in slightly salty brackish water. An exception is the guppy, which comes from soft-water streams in eastern South America. Guppies and

Top: Platys (*Xiphophorus maculatus*) are bred in different forms.

Bottom: Fan-tailed guppy (*poecilia reticulata*).

Swordtails (*Xiphophorus helleri*) like to swim free in a large tank.

mosquito fish mainly eat various plankton, but also some vegetable food. The Asiatic halfbeak lurks directly under the water surface, waiting for insects. The other species eat algae, which they pick directly from hard surfaces with their pointed mouths.

Reproduction: All the described species bear completely developed fry. Generally, the fry are still enclosed by an egg membrane in the mother's body.

Just before birth, they hatch out of the eggs while still in the mother's body. In a planted, not too densely populated, aquarium, some fry always survive. To increase the yield, a pregnant, very fat female is carefully put into a small, thickly planted tank or a special breeding tank (available in the pet store) until the young are born. After that, the mother is placed back in the maintenance tank so that she does not eat her young. The fry eat finely grated dry food immediately after birth.

Sexing: Males are smaller and more colorful than females. They have a penis-like anal fin.

Care: Light, roomy tanks with medium-hard to hard water offer the best conditions. Here, also, algae develop, which contributes to a well-balanced diet for most species. A salt supplement (2 teaspoons per 5 gallons [19 L]) is important for sailfin mollies and black mollies. All live-bearers are social. Therefore, there should be at least five fish kept of any species. It is good if there are more females, so that the individual females are not pursued too vigorously by the males.

Planting the aquarium offers the females protection and also allows fry to survive by hiding among the plants.

Diet: Live-bearers can be adequately fed with dry food containing a high portion of vegetable matter. Regular feeding with live food (water fleas, cyclops, small gnat larvae) increases vitality. Strong lighting provides for good algae growth. Halfbeaks need fruit flies or other small insects in order to thrive.

Live-Bearing Fish

Fish Species	Size	Tank	Water Type	Temperature	Photo
Guppy *Poecilia reticulata*	2¹/2 in (6 cm)	16 in (40 cm)	2–5	75–86°F (24–30°C)	pages 92–93, 24
Black molly *Poecilia sphenops* var.	3–4³/4 in (8–12 cm)	32 in (80 cm)	5–6	79–84°F (26–29°C)	page 26 top
Sailfin molly *Poecilia velifera*	6 in (15 cm)	47 in (120 cm)	6	77–82°F (25–28°C)	page 26 bottom
Swordtail *Xiphophorus helleri*	4³/4 in (12 cm)	39 in (100 cm)	5–6	72–82°F (22–28°C)	page 25
Platy *Xiphophorus maculatus*	2¹/2 in (6 cm)	24 in (60 cm)	5–6	69–77°F (21–25°C)	page 24 top
Platy *Xiphophorus variatus*	2¹/2 in (6 cm)	24 in (60 cm)	5–6	72–77°F (22–25°C)	page 26 center
Mosquito fish *Heterandria formosa*	1¹/2 in (4 cm)	16 in (40 cm)	5–6	64–86°F (18–30°C)	
Halfbeak *Dermogenys* sp.	2³/4 in (7 cm)	32 in (80 cm)	5–6	75–82°F (24–28°C)	

Top: Black mollies (*Poecilia sphenops* var.) are susceptible to disease at lower temperatures.

Center: The variatus platy (*Xiphophorus variatus*).

Bottom: Sailfin mollies (*Poecilia velifera*) love a vegetable diet.

Combination: Can be combined with all bottom-oriented or other peaceable, schooling fishes of the middle- and upper-tank regions that tolerate hard, alkaline water. They also go well with not-too-large Central American cichlids. In densely planted tanks, halfbeaks and mosquito fish can also live with species that remain small.

27

Rainbow Fish and Silversides

The lively rainbow fish and their relatives are "children of the morning sun." They show their most intense colors and behave the liveliest in the morning hours.

Distinguishing marks: In contrast to other school fish, the rainbow fish and silversides have two dorsal fins but no adipose fin.

Habits in the wild: All species noted in the table live in clear streams, rivers, or lakes with dense plant growth in Australia, New Guinea, and Sulawesi. There they feed on plankton and insects or nibble on algae.

Reproduction: Rainbow fish deposit relatively large eggs primarily on plants. They do not care for their young.

Sexing: Adult males are characteristically more colorful than females.

Care: These extremely active fish need spacious aquariums with much free swimming area but also with dense plant growth. All species feel comfortable in well-lighted tanks and should be kept in a group.

Diet: High-quality dry food containing greens is an appropriate basic diet. Supplements of live or

Top: Celebes rainbow fish (*Telmatherina ladigesi*).

Left: Red rainbow fish (*Glossolepis incisus*).

28

Pseudomugil furcatus.

frozen brine shrimp or cyclops are recommended.

Combination: With bottom-oriented fish or other lively fish that have the same water and light requirements. *Iriatherina* should be kept alone or only with other delicate species.

Rainbow Fish and Silversides

Fish Species	Size	Tank	Water Type	Temperature	Photo
Dwarf rainbow fish *Melanotaenia praecox*	2¹/₂ in (6 cm)	32 in (80 cm)	2–5	73–82°F (23–28°C)	pages 62–63
Boeseman's rainbow fish *Melanotaenia boesemani*	5¹/₂ in (14 cm)	47 in (120 cm)	5–6	73–79°F (23–26°C)	
Red rainbow fish *Glossolepis incisus*	6 in (15 cm)	47 in (120 cm)	5–6	72–77°F (22–25°C)	page 28 bottom
Threadfin rainbow fish *Iriatherina werneri*	2 in (5 cm)	24 in (60 cm)	2–6	77–81°F (25–27°C)	page 121
Pseudomugil furcatus	2¹/₂ in (6 cm)	24 in (60 cm)	2–5	75–81°F (24–27°C)	page 29
Celebes rainbow fish *Telmatherina ladigesi*	2³/₄ in (7 cm)	32 in (80 cm)	5–6	77–82°F (25–28°C)	page 28 top

Catfish

Droll armored catfish and mailed catfish are at home in almost any community tank. Not only are they useful as "clean-up crew" and algae-eaters, they also create an interesting contrast to colorful fish in open water. Catfish do, however, have their own particular habitat requirements.

Distinguishing marks: Catfish do not have scales but are either naked (*Synodontis schoutedeni*, glass catfish, and *pictus* catfish) or covered with bony plates (armored catfish, mailed catfish). There are barbels on the mouth, which in species with a suck-

ing mouth (especially *Synodontis schoutedeni*) are very small.

Habits in the wild: Most species live on the bottom and there, depending on the species, feed on different food sources. Armored catfish in South American

Top: Sterba's corydoras (*Corydoras sterbai*).

Left: The cuckoo catfish (*Synodontis multipunctatus*) gets its eggs brooded by cichlids (see page 104).

Dwarf catfish (*Corydoras hastatus*) like to swim in open water.

Right: Bronze catfish (*Corydoras aeneus*) like to burrow in the mulm, organic sediment that collects in the aquarium.

nocturnal and are thus more comfortable at night or in cloudy water with little light. By means of their barbels (especially long in the Peruvian *pictus* catfish) catfish can feel their environment and even taste it.

Reproduction: The rainy season is the mating season for most catfish. As far as we know, all species lay relatively large, adhesive eggs, which are brooded by the male.

Sexing: Not always easy to tell apart. Adult males are more slender than the females. In many, but not all, mailed catfish, males develop imposing growths on the head (*Ancistrus*).

Care: Even if catfish are only being kept as "garbage men," they still have their own special requirements that should not be overlooked. For the sociable armored catfish,

streams and rivers feed on small insect larvae and worms. The mailed catfish, also South American, feed on algae or the small animals that live among the algae, scraping up the food with their toothed sucking mouth. Only the dwarf catfish and the Asiatic glass catfish live among plants in the open areas of quiet bodies of water, where they eat water fleas and other small creatures. Many species, like the African *Synodontis schoutedeni* are a soft bottom of sand or fine, round pebbles is especially important so that when they burrow in the substrate their sensitive barbels are not injured. All species need places to rest. The sociable glass catfish, armored catfish, and *otocinclus* (keep at least five of a species together!) like dense plant growth. With all the other species, branching roots and caves provide hiding places for each individual animal, protecting it from aggressive fellow species members. The constantly circling *pictus* catfish needs no resting place and in fact loves the company of fish of different species. It's best to offer the Tanganyikan *Synodontis schoutedeni* a stone cave because wooden roots make the water acidic. All species like dim light.

Diet: Even though catfish clean up many leftovers in the aquarium, they still need additional food; otherwise, they slowly starve to death. It's best to feed them in the evening shortly before turning off the lights because the catfish can then look for their food undisturbed by the other fish. Dry food tablets serve as a basic diet for almost all catfish species (except for glass catfish).

Regal whiptails (*Sturisoma* sp.) during spawning.

Left top: *Acistrus hoplogenys*.

Left center: Peppered corydoras (*Corydoras paleatus*).

Left bottom: Upside-down catfish (*Synodontis nigriventris*).

But for the algae-eaters (*Ancistrus, Otocinclus*), vegetable food rich in roughage is imperative: Scalded lettuce leaves, pieces of potato, or almost any other vegetable will be accepted. Glass catfish need small live food especially brine shrimp and cyclops. Frozen microcrustaceans should be on the menu for all species now and then.

Combination: The species included here can be kept easily with schooling fish of the upper and middle water layers such as characins, barbs, and live-bearers. All tankmates should have the same requirements for water quality as the catfish. With catfish, you only need to differentiate from other bottom-oriented species when making up combinations.

Armored catfish and cich-lids cancel each other out because they are mutually disturbing to one another. Small mailed catfish (*Otocinclus, Hypancistrus zebra, Rineloricaria*) and dwarf cichlids, on the other hand, are a good combina-tion. Larger mailed catfish (*Ancistrus dolichopterus* but not regal whiptails and *Synodontis schoutedeni*) can also be kept with larger cichlids if there are enough hiding places available in the tank. Glass catfish and the dwarf catfish are recom-mended for a community of robust, lively species.

Top: *Otocinclus* catfish are good algae controllers for small aquariums.

Bottom: Bristle-mouth or blue-chin catfish (*Ancistrus dolichopterus*).

34

Catfish

Fish Species	Size	Tank	Water Type	Temperature	Photo
Bronze corydoras *Corydoras aeneus*	2^1/$_2$ in (6 cm)	20 in (50 cm)	2–6	77–82°F (25–28°C)	page 31 bottom
Peppered corydoras *Corydoras paleatus*	2^3/$_4$ in (7 cm)	24 in (60 cm)	2–6	64–73°F (18–23°C)	page 32 center
Sterba's corydoras *Corydoras sterbai*	2^1/$_2$ in (6 cm)	20 in (50 cm)	2–5	72–77°F (22–25°C)	page 30 top
Dwarf catfish *Corydoras hastatus*	1 in (2.5 cm)	16 in (40 cm)	2–6	77–82°F (25–28°C)	page 31 top
Golden otocinclus *Otocinclus affinis*	1^1/$_2$ in (4 cm)	16 in (40 cm)	2–6	72–79°F (22–26°C)	page 34 top
Zebra catfish *Hypancistrus zebra*	3 in (8 cm)	20 in (50 cm)	2–5	81–86°F (27–30°C)	back cover
Whiptails *Rineloricaria sp.*	5 in (13 cm)	24 in (60 cm)	2–5	75–82°F (24–28°C)	
Bristle-mouth catfish *Ancistrus dolichopterus*	6 in (15 cm)	32 in (80 cm)	2–5	77–82°F (25–28°C)	page 34 bottom
Regal whiptails *Sturisoma sp.*	10 in (25 cm)	47 in (120 cm)	2–5	77–84°F (25–29°C)	page 33
Glass catfish *Kryptopterus minor*	2^3/$_4$ in (7 cm)	32 in (80 cm)	2–5	75–82°F (24–28°C)	
Marbled synodontis *Synodontis schoutedeni*	6^3/$_4$ in (17 cm)	47 in (120 cm)	2–5	77–82°F (25–28°C)	page 127
Angelic catfish *Synodontis angelicus*	10 in (25 cm)	59 in (150 cm)	2–5	75–82°F (24–28°C)	
Cuckoo catfish *Synodontis multipunctatus*	4^3/$_4$ in (12 cm)	47 in (120 cm)	5–6	77–81°F (25–27°C)	page 30 bottom
Upside-down catfish *Synodontis nigriventris*	3^3/$_4$ in (10 cm)	32 in (80 cm)	2–5	75–82°F (24–28°C)	page 32 bottom
Pictus catfish *Pimelodus pictus*	4^3/$_4$ in (12 cm)	47 in (120 cm)	2–5	77–82°F (25–28°C)	

Cichlids in General

Characteristics: In contrast to other perch-like fish, cichlids have an undivided dorsal fin with spines and with soft rays. They have one nostril on each side of the head.

Habits in the wild: Cichlids inhabit varied habitats, from fast currents to hot springs, in tropcal fresh waters of the Americas, Africa, and India.

Reproduction: All species take care of their young. The so-called substrate brooders lay many small eggs on wood, stone, or leaves in their territory. Both parents or only one care for the eggs and the fry for several weeks and defend their territory. Most substrate brooders form pairs or harems (one male with several females), which remain together for a long time. Mouthbrooders, on the other hand, only rarely form permanent pairs. They take the eggs into their mouth directly after spawning, or the fry at a later point in time, and can thus carry the brood around with them. Here too, the distribution of roles varies according to species.

Combination: At least during the reproduction period, all species defend their territory.

Other fish species are then driven away, although previously there was enough space available for all.

Dwarf Cichlids

These small cichlids only grow 4 in (10 cm), which makes them particularly suited for community tanks.

Habits in the wild: Most dwarf cichlids inhabit shallow, riparian areas with plants, dead wood, and fallen

Right top: *Pseudocrenilabrus nicholsi*, a mouthbrooder from Zaire.

Right bottom: *Apistogramma reitzigi*.

Below: From South America, the ram or butterfly dwarf cichlid (*Microgeophagus ramirezi*).

leaves. There they look for insect larvae, among other things.

Care and reproduction: Keep substrate brooders in pairs (*Anomalochromis* and *Pelvicachromis* from West Africa, *Laetacara* and *Microgeophagus* from South America) or a male with several females (*Apistogramma* and *Dicrossus* from South America, *Nanochromis* from Central Africa, Egyptian mouthbrooders from East Africa) in planted tanks. Some fry will often survive in planted aquariums that are not too densely populated.

Top: *Discrossus filamentosus* swim among the leaves of aquarium plants.

Bottom: Curviceps cichlid (*Laetacara curviceps*).

Fry should be given supplementary feedings of brine shrimp nauplii.

Sexing: Males are larger. In *Pelvicachromis* and *Nanochromis* species, the females are more colorful.

Diet: Small dry, live, and frozen food.

Combination: With non-territorial, small fish of the middle- and upper-tank regions.

Pelvicachromis taeniatus.

Dwarf Cichlids

Fish Species	Size	Tank	Water Type	Temperature	Photo
Agassiz's dwarf cichlid *Apistogramma agassizii*	4 in (10 cm)	32 in (80 cm)	1–3	79–84°F (26–29°C)	
Cockatoo dwarf cichlid *Apistogramma cacatuoides*	3¹/₂ in (9 cm)	32 in (80 cm)	2–6	79–84°F (26–29°C)	page 99
Apistogramma reitzigi	2¹/₂ in (6 cm)	20 in (50 cm)	2–5	75–79°F (24–26°C)	page 37 bottom
Dicrossus filamentosus	3¹/₂ in (9 cm)	32 in (80 cm)	1–2	77–84°F (25–29°C)	page 38 top
Curviceps cichlid *Laetacara curviceps*	3 in (8 cm)	24 in (60 cm)	2–5	79–86°F (26–30°C)	page 38 bottom
Ram or **butterfly dwarf cichlid** *Microgeophagus ramirezi*	2 in (5 cm)	20 in (50 cm)	1–3	81–86°F (27–30°C)	page 104
*Anomalochromis thomasi**	3 in (8 cm)	24 in (60 cm)	2–5	75–82°F (24–28°C)	
Kribensis cichlid *Pelvicachromis pulcher*	4 in (10 cm)	32 in (80 cm)	2–5	77–82°F (25–28°C)	
*Pelvicachromis taeniatus**	3¹/₄ in (8.5 cm)	24 in (60 cm)	2–5	77–82°F (25–28°C)	page 39
*Pseudocrenilabrus nicholsi**	3 in (8 cm)	32 in (80 cm)	3–6	73–79°F (23–26°C)	page 37 top
Egyptian mouthbrooder *Pseudocrenilabrus multicolor*	3 in. (8 cm)	32 in (80 cm)	3–6	73–81°F (23–27°C)	page 118
Nanochromis cichlid *Nanochromis transvestitus**	2¹/₂ in (6 cm)	20 in (50 cm)	1–3	81–84°F (27–29°C)	pages 108–109

*Not commonly available in the United States.

Angelfish and Discus

The kings of the tropical fish from the Amazon are less demanding in care than their reputation leads one to expect. Still, there are some essential basic requirements.

Habits in the wild: In nature, all species are social animals that live in groups of several dozen individuals. The most common resting place of such groups is between the branches of fallen trees, but they may also shelter between rocks. Single pairs must be kept separate for breeding. They feed on insect larvae, small freshwater shrimp, and worms.

Care and reproduction: Both angelfish and discus need roomy tanks at least 20 in (50 cm) high. In such an aquarium, they can be kept in accordance with their natural lifestyle in groups of six to eight. Tangled driftwood, dark tank substrate, and diffuse lighting imitate their natural conditions. Planting with large rosette plants that let little light through (such as *Echinodorus* species) completes the picture. With appropriate water values, the fish will also spawn in the aquarium on pieces of a root or a leaf. In thinly populated tanks, the fascinating brood care of the discus fish can then be observed: The fry feed for a time on the body mucus of the parents before they later switch over to brine shrimp nauplii.

Sexing: Differences are scarcely recognizable. The pointed spawning papilla of the male can only be recognized shortly before egg laying. The best way to obtain a mated pair is to buy several small specimens of the type in which you are interested and rear them together in the same aquarium. When they mature, the fish will form pairs on their own. Purchasing a mated pair may be faster, but often there is no way to tell if the fish are robust, young specimens, or an aging pair near the end of their breeding lives.

Diet: Besides good water quality, the right diet is

Angelfish (*Pterophyllum scalare*) live in groups and need tanks at least 20 in (50 cm) high.

40

The discus (*Symphysodon aequifasciata*) comes in different color combinations.

able commercially and it is also good for angelfish. These mixtures should, however, contain no beef heart and no milk products (read the contents on the package). The special food can be fed exclusively. For a change in the menu, add frozen small shrimp, cyclops, and small mosquito larvae.

Note: Avoid *Tubifex* and bloodworms as food animals, because their pesticide-free origins cannot be guaranteed.

Combination: Quiet characins, dwarf cichlids, mailed catfish, and armored catfish can be put with discus and angelfish without any problems as long as the peaceful character of the aquarium is maintained. **Caution:** Angelfish sometimes eat small, slender characins.

the most important care measure, because animals that are fed an incorrect or unbalanced diet quickly become sick. Dry and frozen food that is especially developed for discus fish is avail-

Angelfish and Discus

Fish Species	Size	Tank	Water Type	Temperature	Photo
Angelfish *Pterophyllum scalare*	6 in (15 cm)	32 in (80 cm)	2–5	75–82°F (24–28°C)	pages 40, 96–97
*Pterophyllum altum**	7 in (18 cm)	47 in (120 cm)	1–2	81–84°F (27–29°C)	page 117
Discus *Symphysodon aequifasciata*	7 in (18 cm)	47 in (120 cm)	2–4	81–86°F (27–30°C)	page 41

*Extremely rare in the United States.

Larger Cichlids

Popular species are between 4 and 12 in (10 and 30 cm) long.

Habits in the wild: Convict cichlids and firemouth cichlids come from the clear brooks of Central America and primarily feed on insect larvae, but also on plant food. The quiet but large *Heros* and festive cichlids occupy the middle and upper regions of quiet South American water bodies with much structure (dead wood, water plants). Among the three Africans, the aggressive jewel cichlids are also the most adaptable, for they inhabit both the cloudy savannah waters and clear rain forest streams. The *Steatocranus* live exclusively on the rocky floor of the fast-flowing lower Congo.

Chromidotilapia finleyi are African rain forest specialists with a preference for clear brooks.

Care and reproduction: All species need tanks with plenty of structure in which the subordinate animals can also take shelter. Therefore, stone caves and slabs are most suitable. The substrate-brooders lay their eggs there; the pair-forming *Chromidotilapia finleyi*

takes turns caring for the young with its partner.

Sexing: Males are bigger, sometimes with a head boss.

Diet: Fiber-rich dry food and sturdy live and frozen food.

Combination: Only in large aquariums with medium-size to large, peaceful fish.

Top: Firemouth cichlid (*Thorichthys meeki*).

Bottom: From Central America, the convict cichlid (*Archocentrus nigrofasciatus*) prefers hard water.

Festive cichlids (*Mesonauta insignis*) live in the upper regions of the tank.

Larger Cichlids

Fish Species	Size	Tank	Water Type	Temperature	Photo
Convict cichlid *Archocentrus nigrofasciatus*	6 in (15 cm)	39 in (100 cm)	5–6	73–81°F (23–27°C)	page 42 bottom
Firemouth cichlid *Thorichthys meeki*	6 in (15 cm)	39 in (100 cm)	3–6	75–81°F (24–27°C)	page 42 top
Festive cichlids *Mesonauta* sp.	up to 8 in. (20 cm)	from 47 in (120 cm)	2–5	79–86°F (26–30°C)	page 43 top
Hero cichlids *Heros* sp.	up to 12 in (30 cm)	from 47 in (120 cm)	2–5	77–84°F (25–29°C)	
Jewel cichlid red *Hemichromis* sp.	4$\frac{1}{3}$ in (11 cm)	39 in (100 cm)	2–6	75–84°F (24–29°C)	
Steatocranus casuarius*	5$\frac{1}{2}$ in (14 cm)	32 in (80 cm)	3–6	75–82°F (24–28°C)	
Chromidotilapia finleyi*	4 in (10 cm)	32 in (80 cm)	2–5	75–81°F (24–27°C)	

*Rare in the United States.

Tanganyika Cichlids

Several hundred cichlid species live exclusively in East African Lake Tanganyika.

Habits in the wild: All the species named live in the countless rock ledges that line the banks of the lake. Only the snail cichlids have given up the protection of the cracks in the rocks. In the course of evolution, they have so changed their form that they find shelter in the many empty snail shells that are strewn over the lake bottom. All species feed on small crabs and insect larvae.

Care and reproduction: Snail cichlids (*Neolamprologus, Lamprologus*) need only some empty snail shells for protection and spawning; these should lie on a layer of fine sand. For breeding caves, the other species should instead be offered piles of rocks with many horizontal and vertical fissures so that every animal has a place into which to withdraw.

Sexing: The male becomes larger than the female (except for the julies).

Diet: A mixture of dry food and deep-frozen crustaceans and live brine shrimp has proved good.

Combination: In large tanks, with other Tanganyika cichlids or schooling fish that remain small and tolerate hard, alkaline water. An important key to the successful care of Tanganyika cichlids is to maintain clean conditions by performing regular partial water changes.

Above: From Tanganyika, *Neolamprologus leleupi.*

Among the julies (*Julidochromis regani*), the female is often larger than the male.

Left bottom: This daffodil-yellow Tanganyika cichlid is closely related to *Neolamprologus brichardi*.

Tanganyika Cichlids

Fish Species	Size	Tank	Water Type	Temperature	Photo
Neolamprologus brichardi	6 in (15 cm)	39 in (100 cm)	5–6	77–81°F (25–27°C)	page 44 bottom
Neolamprologus multifasciatus	2 in (5 cm)	20 in (50 cm)	5–6	77–81°F (25–27°C)	
Neolamprologus leleupi/ N. longior	$4^{1}/_{3}$ in (11 cm)	32 in (80 cm)	5–6	77–81°F (25–27°C)	page 44 top
Lamprologus ocellatus	2 in (5 cm)	24 in (60 cm)	5–6	77–81°F (25–27°C)	
Julidochromis regani	$4^{3}/_{4}$ in (12 cm)	32 in (80 cm)	5–6	77–81°F (25–27°C)	page 45 top
Altolamprologus compressiceps	$5^{1}/_{2}$ in (14 cm)	39 in (100 cm)	5–6	77–81°F (25–27°C)	

Malawi Cichlids

The cichlids of the East African Lake Malawi are also called freshwater coral fish. With their bright colors, they certainly live up to this name.

Habits in the wild: Most of the species commonly kept in aquariums come from the rock regions of the more than 435-mile (700-km)-long Lake Malawi. The species of the genera *Pseudotropheus, Melanochromis,* and *Labidochromis* graze on the algae and the live food animals in it in the sun-dappled waters of the rock surfaces. But they also eat small crustaceans in the open waters. Altogether they are called "Mbuna." On the other hand, *Aulonocara* species are quiet inhabitants of shadowy caves and hunt small animals buried in the sand.

Sciaenochromis is a predatory sand dweller.

Care and reproduction: All Malawi cichlids are mouthbrooders. The female carries the eggs. The colorful males defend territory into which they court females and spawn with them. But the pair does not stay together. A single male should always be kept with several females

so that single females are not too severely harried.

Sexing: The male is more colorful. Males have egg spots, which imitate the eggs of the females.

Diet: Dry food with plant content; microcrustaceans (*Artemia, Mysis,* cyclops).

Combination: The aggressive Mbuna may be kept with other peaceful Malawi species only in very large aquariums from 59 in (150 cm). Other possible tankmates might include one or more species of the synodontid catfishes that also call Lake Malawi home.

Above: The females of *Melanochromis johannii* are orange, in contrast to the male pictured.

Labidochromis spp. "yellow" are among the most popular Malawi cichlids.

Left, bottom: *Aulonocara jacobfreibergi* need a quiet community.

Cichlids of Lakes Malawi and Victoria

Fish species	Size	Tank	Water Type	Temperature	Photo
Melanochromis johannii	3¹/₂ in (9 cm)	39 in (100 cm)	5–6	77–82°F (25–28°C)	page 46 top
Pseudotropheus sp.	2³/₄ to 5 in (7 to 13 cm)	39 to 47 in (100 to 120 cm)	5–6	77–82°F (25–28°C)	page 110
Sciaenochromis freyeri	6³/₄ in (17 cm)	59 in (150 cm)	5–6	77–82°F (25–28°C)	page 114
Peacocks *Aulonocara jacobfreibergi*	5 in (13 cm)	39 in (100 cm)	5–6	77–82°F (25–28°C)	page 46 bottom
Labidochromis spp. "yellow"	4 in (10 cm)	39 in (100 cm)	5–6	77–82°F (25–28°C)	page 47
*Iodotropheus sprengerae**	4¹/₃ in (11 cm)	39 in (100 cm)	5–6	77–82°F (25–28°C)	

*Uncommon in the United States and costly when available.

47

Killifish

Distinguishing marks: Long, colorful fish with a flat back.

Habits in the wild: Most species live singly in the rain forest brooks of Africa (*Aphyosemion*, *Epiplatys*), South America (*Rivulus*), or Asia (*Aplocheilus*), where they lurk under cover of the fallen leaves to hunt for insects. Lamp-eyes are insect-eating fish that school in the open water of clear rain forest brooks.

Reproduction: Spawn is deposited on various substrates; no brood care.

Sexing: The males are larger and more colorful.

Care: Dark tanks, structured with plants and roots, offer the best possibilities for creating small territories. Lamp-eyes need companions of the same species, space to swim in, and a slight current.

Diet: Fruit flies, gnat larvae, and brine shrimp. Some can get used to dry or frozen food.

Combination: With fish of the same size, not too lively school fish, or small catfish. No cichlids.

Killifish*

Fish Species	Size	Tank	Water Type	Temperature	Photo
Steel-blue killi *Aphyosemion gardneri*	2³/4 in (7 cm)	20 in (50 cm)	2–4	73–81°F (23–27°C)	pages 6–7
Aphyosemion striatum	2 in (5 cm)	16 in (40 cm)	2–5	70–73°F (21–23°C)	page 48 top
Lyre-tail killifish *Aphyosemion australe*	2¹/2 in (6 cm)	16 in (40 cm)	2–4	70–75°F (21–24°C)	page 48 center
Nigerian (yellow) lamp-eye *Procatopus similis*	2¹/2 in (6 cm)	32 in (80 cm)	2–5	72–77°F (22–25°C)	page 48 bottom
Dwarf (red) lamp-eye *Aplocheilichthys macrophthalmus*	1¹/2 in (4 cm)	16 in (40 cm)	2–5	77–82°F (25–28°C)	
Sparkling panchax *Apolcheilus lineatus*	4³/4 in (12 cm)	32 in (80 cm)	2–6	75–84°F (24–29°C)	page 49
Orange-throated panchax *Epiplatys dageti monroviae*	2¹/2 in (6 cm)	20 in (50 cm)	2–5	73–79°F (23–26°C)	
Rivulus (blue-striped brookling) *Rivulus xiphidius*	1¹/2 in (4 cm)	16 in (40 cm)	2	73–77°F (23–25°C)	page 124

*Killifish are usually not sold in U.S. aquarium stores, but fish and their eggs are avidly traded by enthusiasts (see Useful Addresses, page 125).

Left, top: *Aphyosemion striatum*.

Left, center: Lyre-tail killifish (*Aphyosemion australe*).

Left, bottom: Nigerian lamp-eye (*Procatopus similis*).

Right: Golden sparkling panchaxes (*Aplocheilus lineatus*).

Labyrinth Fish

Distinguishing marks: They have an additional respiratory organ, the labyrinth, which is not visible from the outside.

Habits in the wild: All species feed on plankton in standing or slightly flowing waters of Southeast Asia with dense plant growth. (Only the *Microtenopoma* come from Africa.)

Reproduction: The males of the species here named build a bubble nest on the upper surface of the water, in which, after he has embraced his partner,

the eggs are laid and are then cared for and defended by the male in the first days after hatching.

Sexing: Males are more colorful and usually larger.

Care: Densely planted, dark tanks without any current. Keeping a pair is ideal. Only keep several males in large tanks.

Diet: Dry food, occasionally live food.

Combination: Quiet school fish and ground dwellers. No cichlids.

Above: The honey gourami (*Colisa chuna*) is the smallest gourami.

Left: Paradise fish (*Macropodus opercularis*) are among the aquarium fish with the "highest seniority."

Sparkling gouramis (*Trichopsis pumilus*) can make a growling sound.

Labyrinth Fish

Fish Species	Size	Tank	Water Type	Temperature	Photo
Siamese fighting fish *Betta splendens*	2¹/₃ in (6 cm)	20 in (50 cm)	2–6	73–82°F (23–28°C)	pages 4–5, front cover, small photo
Sparkling gourami* *Trichopsis pumilus*	1¹/₂ in (4 cm)	16 in (40 cm)	2–6	73–81°F (23–27°C)	page 51
Honey gourami *Colisa chuna*	1³/₄ in (4.5 cm)	20 in (50 cm)	2–6	72–82°F (22–28°C)	page 50 top
Dwarf gourami *Colisa lalia*	2¹/₃ in (6 cm)	24 in (60 cm)	2–6	75–82°F (24–28°C)	page 59
Lace (pearl) gourami *Trichogaster leeri*	4³/₄ in (12 cm)	39 in (100 cm)	2–4	77–84°F (25–29°C)	front cover, large photo
Three-spot (blue) gourami *Trichogaster trichopterus*	4³/₄ in (12 cm)	39 in (100 cm)	2–6	72–81°F (22–27°C)	page 87
Paradise fish *Macropodus opercularis*	4 in (10 cm)	32 in (80 cm)	2–6	68–79°F (20–26°C)	page 50 bottom
Microtenopoma ansorgii*	2³/₄ in (7 cm)	24 in (60 cm)	2–5	73–81°F (23–27°C)	

*Not common in the United States.

Fish from Other Groups

Both goby species from Southeast Asia and New Guinea can be kept in groups of several in very small tanks. Wasp gobies, being brackish water fishes, need a salt supplement (uniodized table salt without any additives; 4 tsp per 5 gal [19 L]). Do not combine this fish with other species!

The dwarf perch from Southeast Asia is cared for like the labyrinth fish, but the males do not build a bubble nest. Do not feed any live food.

The Indian glassfish from Asia is a schooling fish that is fed with cyclops and brine shrimp. Put together with small, delicate fish.

The *Macrognathus aculeatus* from Southeast Asia lead a secretive life in a tank rich in structures. They can be fed with various frozen foods.

The *Eigenmannia virescens* lives in groups in the Amazon under a cover of floating plants, which it also needs in the aquarium. Only put together with bottom-dwellers, but no cichlids. Feed a variety of live and frozen food.

The Peter's elephant nose from African streams can, like the *Eigenmannia virescens*,

Left, top: Wasp goby (*Brachygobius doriae*).

Left, bottom: Freshwater butterfly fish (*Pantodon buchholzi*).

Right, top: Peter's elephant nose (*Gnathonemus petersi*).

African knife fish (*Xenomystus nigri*).

sense its environment with weak electric discharges and so communicate with others of its species. These animals, which are nocturnal and aggressive with one another, withdraw during the day into their hiding places (for instance, clay pipes). No dry food; feed at night with rinsed *Tubifex*.

The African knife fish from West Africa lives in waters filled with reeds. Care is like that for Peter's elephant nose. Feed with large living food.

The freshwater butterfly fish from West African swamps eats large insects from the water surface, both in the wild and in the aquarium.

Keep with quiet fish of the lower regions that like shadows made by floating plants. Don't use any dry food.

The *Carinotetraodon lorteti* from Asia loves plant-filled tanks and feeds exclusively on live food, primarily small snails. Don't put with other species!

The reed fish from West Africa is a swamp dweller that lives sociably on the bottom in a heavily planted aquarium with many hiding places. Make the aquarium escape-proof! Feed coarse live and frozen food.

The *Achirus* species from South America need a sandy bottom on which they will not be disturbed by other bottom-dwellers. If necessary, feed at night so that the fish will be able to get food.

Top: Indian glassfish (*Chanda ranga*).

Center: *Eigenmannia virescens*.

Bottom: Reed fish (*Erpetoichthys calabaricus*).

Fish from Other Groups

Fish Species	Size	Tank	Water Type	Temperature	Photo
Wasp goby *Brachygobius doriae*	1¹/₃ in (3.5 cm)	16 in (40 cm)	5–6	81–86°F (27–30°C)	page 52 top
Peacock or **eye-spot sleeper goby** *Tateurndina ocellicauda*	2 in (5 cm)	16 in (40 cm)	2–5	79–84°F (26–29°C)	page 73
Dwarf (blue) perch *Badis badis*	2¹/₃ in (6 cm)	20 in (50 cm)	2–6	77–82°F (25–28°C)	
Indian glassfish *Chandra ranga*	2 in (5 cm)	20 in (50 cm)	5–6	77–84°F (25–29°C)	page 54 top
Macrognathus aculeatus	10 in (25 cm)	39 in (100 cm)	2–5	75–82°F (24–28°C)	pages 76–77
Eigenmannia virescens	14 in (35 cm)	59 in (150 cm)	2–5	77–84°F (25–29°C)	page 54 center
Peter's elephant nose *Gnathonemus petersi*	9 in (23 cm)	47 in (120 cm)	2–5	75–82°F (24–28°C)	page 53 top
Freshwater butterfly fish *Pantodon buchholzi*	4³/₄ in (12 cm)	39 in (100 cm)	2–5	81–86°F (27–30°C)	page 52 bottom
African knife fish *Xenomystus nigri*	9 in (23 cm)	59 in (150 cm)	2–5	79–84°F (26–29°C)	page 53 bottom
Carinotetraodon lorteti	2¹/₃ in (6 cm)	20 in (50 cm)	2–4	75–82°F (24–28°C)	page 100
Reed fish *Erpetoichthys calabaricus*	14¹/₂ in (37 cm)	39 in (100 cm)	2–5	79–84°F (26–29°C)	page 54 bottom
Achirus sp.	4 in (10 cm)	24 in (60 cm)	2–5	79–84°F (26–29°C)	

Maintenance and proper care

Splendid color and vitality
in your fish are the most reliable signs
that you are providing optimal
maintenance conditions.

Water, the Life Element

The quality of the aquarium water determines the quality of life of the tropical fish that live in it. For the fish not to become sick, the aquarium water must always be clean and must be kept at the tolerable water values for the fish in question.

Water quality is the key to a healthy captive environment for your fish.

Water Has Many Qualities

Every water creature needs a particular "cocktail" of substances dissolved in the water to feel its best.

The most important factors for water quality in the aquarium are the content of biological waste products (especially nitrate), the content of so-called hardening constituents (water hardness), the degree of acidity (pH value), and the content of the dissolved gases oxygen and carbon dioxide. Because these substances cannot be seen with the naked eye, their presense is measured with simple chemical tests from the pet store. Using the test results, you can firmly establish if and how the water must be changed so that it will be suitable for the aquarium.

Pathway of Biological Waste Products in the Aquarium

Toxic biological waste products are introduced into the aquarium water through the urine and feces of the fish, rotting remains of food, and dead animals and plants. They are broken down by means of the useful bacteria in the soil, in water, and above all in the aquarium filter in a chemical chain reaction to an end product, nitrate (NO_3). To be sure, the water plants use nitrate as fertilizer and thus remove it from the water, but normally their growth needs are not sufficient to keep the nitrate value low. Nitrate must thus be regularly removed from the water.

Nitrate (NO_3) Measurement and Removal

You can measure the nitrate content simply and quickly with test kits available from the pet store. Values under 20 mg/L are ideal. When values are over 50 mg/L, the nitrate must be removed from the aquarium by changing the water. The best thing to do is use a mixture of distilled—and thus nitrate-free—water with tap water (see How to

Dwarf gouramis (*Colisa lalia*) build bubble nests on the water surface.

Rain forest brook in the low-lands of Cameroon. Aquarium water should be just as clear and unpolluted.

Solve Maintenance Problems, beginning on page 112).

Water Hardness

Tap water can have different degrees of hardness, depending on where you live.

Hardness refers to the content of so-called hardening agents. For aquariums, the hardness that is produced by carbonates (so-called carbonate hardness) is especially important. This hardness together with the degree of acidity (pH value) and the car-bon dioxide content form an important triangular relationship in aquarium maintenance.

Carbonate hardness normally constitutes 80 percent of the total hardness and is expressed in "degrees of carbonate hardness" (dKH). When carbonate hardness is subtracted from the total, or general, hardness (dGH), the remainder is called "noncarbonate hardness." Water with lower grades of hardness is called "soft," whereas "hard" water has a higher hardness grade.

Measuring and Altering Water Hardness

Many fish and plants have specific requirements as to water hardness, especially the carbonate hardness. Therefore, you measure the total hardness and carbonate hardness of the tap water with a test kit available from the pet store. It is advisable to do the measuring before the aquarium is set up so that you know which fish and plants can be kept in your tap water.

Lowering water hardness: To decrease the water hardness, tap water is mixed with an appropriate amount of water will all minerals removed by reverse osmosis, or with distilled water purchased in small quantities from the supermarket or drugstore. The right ratio of distilled to tap water is reckoned by means of the "cross rule":

■ Hardness grade of distilled water (0°) minus desired hardness grade gives the portion of distilled water. (Leave out the minus sign!)

■ Hardness grade of tap water minus desired hardness grade gives the portion of tap water.

Example: If you have tap water with a 16° carbonate hardness grade (16 dKH) and would like to produce aquarium water with 4 dKH, mix 12 parts of distilled water with 4 parts of tap water.

Once the water hardness in the aquarium is established, water prepared to the same hardness is used in every water change.

Raising water hardness: Add 3 grams of sodium bicarbonate (baking soda) per 100 L of water to achieve 1 °dKH increase.

The Degree of Acidity (pH Value)

Not only are hardening agents dissolved in water, but acidifying agents are as well.

According to its degree of acidity, water is termed acid, neutral, or alkaline (= basic). The degree of acidity is expressed as the pH value. A pH under 7 indicates acid water. A pH over 7 indicates alkaline water. Water with a pH of 7 is neutral.

Most aquarium fish are comfortable at pH values between 6.5 and 7.5; but some have special requirements.

More important than the pH value itself is the content of the materials that affect the pH. In the aquarium, the pH

Dwarf rainbow fish (*Melanotaenia praecox*) in a small aquarium.

value is determined primarily by carbon dioxide and carbonate hardness agents. These two substances influence each other when they are dissolved in the water: carbon dioxide reacts acidically, carbonates basically. Put simply, high carbonate hardness leads to high pH values, and high carbon dioxide content lowers the pH value. In addition, humic acids, such as those that are contained in peat, lower the pH value.

Measuring pH value: For exact measurement or for electronic pH regulation, electronic pH meters are necessary (see Determining CO_2 Content in Aquarium Water, page 69). So-called continuous pH meters are available in the pet store, but these measure relatively crudely.

Changing pH value: Because the pH is primarily influenced by the carbonate hardness and the carbon dioxide content of the water, it can be altered by the changing of the content of these two substances (see Measuring and Altering Water Hardness, page 61, and Carbon Dioxide, on the next page). An alternative way to change pH is by filtering through peat (see Filter Materials, page 71).

© *Takashi Amano, Aqua Design Amano Co., Ltd.*

Carbon Dioxide (CO$_2$)

This gas, which is found in the air, has two important functions when it is dissolved in aquarium water: For one thing, it is the most important acidifier and thus influences the pH value; for the other, it serves as an important plant nutrient. Plants need carbon to grow with the help of energy-giving light. They take this essential carbon out of the carbon dioxide dissolved in water.

Determining and increasing carbon dioxide content: Because the carbonate hardness and the pH value exist in a chemical relationship with one another, the carbon dioxide content can be determined from these two values (see table, page 69). If you are comparing several CO$_2$ values from the same aquarium, it is important that the measurement always be made at the same time of day, because the values change during the course of

Diamond tetras (*Moenkhausia pittieri*) only develop their full glory of color in clean aquarium water.

Can Fish Drown?

Yes, some fish can actually drown. Fish need oxygen to breathe. Most take it out of the water. But there are also some fish that take oxygen out of the air. Such fish, for example, labyrinth fish, have a special organ for this. It functions something like our lungs. If such a fish is prevented from getting to the water surface to get air, it "drowns." Labyrinth fish often live in warm swamps. There is scarcely any oxygen in the water there. Therefore, to breathe, they must come to the water surface. There are only a few fish that can manage to live in warm swamps.

the day (less CO_2 is used in the morning). For sturdy plant growth, there should be about 15–20 mg/L in the water. The level should not fall below 10 mg/L in a planted aquarium. If necessary, you can use special fertilizing apparatus (see page 72).

Oxygen

Fish and plants need oxygen to breathe. Normally there is always enough oxygen present in the water if the surface is moved by a filter outlet, the tank isn't overpopulated, and there hasn't been overfeeding (rotting food uses oxygen). Also, high temperatures produce a reduction of the oxygen content because in warm water less oxygen is dissolved than in cold.

Good plant growth provides for additional oxygen during the day, because in light, plants break down carbon dioxide freeing oxygen in quantities that are greater than the plants need for their own breathing.

However, at night, the plants use oxygen, as do the fish. When there is an oxygen deficit (fish "stand" in the water sluggishly and breathe rapidly), increase the ventilation, lower the temperature as far as is tolerable for the fish, and remove any rotting materials present.

Technical Equipment For the Aquarium

Unlike nature, the water world in the aquarium is not viable without the intervention of the aquarist. Clear water, the right temperature, sufficient light, and nutrients for fish and plants are provided in the aquarium through the use of technical equipment.

The Glass Tank

The frameless all-glass aquarium, caulked with silicon rubber, has proved to be the best. The pet store offers them in various standard sizes up to a length of about 8 ft (2.4 m). The silicon caulking is very durable, for the rubber is chemically bonded with the glass so that it's as if the two pieces of glass were melted together. In addition, the caulking is flexible and, thus, it gives a little when under slight tension from small unevennesses, which otherwise would lead to the glass breaking.

The choice of color (black or transparent) and type (butted or wraparound) of the caulking has only an aesthetic role in a display aquarium. However, it is important that you buy a tank that is guaranteed to be watertight. This guarantee vouches for careful workmanship.

A natural aquarium with
Rasbora hengeli.

The tank size is determined by the minimum requirements of the fish (see the descriptions section, beginning on page 14) and the space you have available. A basic rule: A larger water volume reacts less sensitively to faulty maintenance. However, 1 qt (1L) of water also weighs about 2 lb (1 kg), for which reason, with large tanks, you must consider the load-bearing capacity of the floor and the stand (possibly ask a structural engineer!). The gallon/liter capacity of an aquarium can be calculated as follows:

length × width × height
in inches / 231 = gallons
in cm / 1000 = liter

A tank of 12 × 12 × 14 in (30 × 30 × 36 cm) thus holds more than 8 gal (32.4 L). The standard commercial sizes offer various widths and heights of tanks of the same length. Bottom-dwelling and territorial fish prefer deeper tanks, whereas the body shapes of the tall fish (for example, angelfish) require tall aquariums. Custom-made tanks are also available.

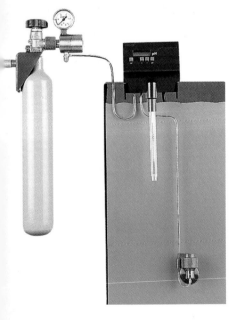

Left: Carbon dioxide fertilizing system with automatic CO$_2$ doser, which is controlled by the pH measuring equipment.

Motorized internal filter with foam cartridge for small aquariums.

Right: A wet/dry external filter provides the filter bacteria with ample oxygen.

Setting Up and Operating a CO_2 System

Step 1:
Measure carbonate hardness of the aquarium water: Choose the desired CO_2 content by locating the tank's carbonate hardness in the table below and determining the pH value that goes with it. This pH value must agree with the requirements of the fish and plants to be kept. If the desired CO_2 value cannot be attained with the measured carbonate hardness in a pH range suitable for the fish, the carbonate hardness must be changed (normally to values between 3° and 12° carbonate hardness).

Step 2:
Mounting the CO_2 equipment: Mount the carbon dioxide system, including the pH tester (color indicator and, with electronic CO_2 regulation, measuring electrode), exactly according to directions that come with it.

Step 3:
For manual pH regulation: Open the vent of the CO_2 bottle slightly so that about 10 bubbles per minute are being counted in the bubble counter. Check the pH after 3 hours; raise the CO_2 feed to a higher value or lower it. Repeat measurements at 3-hour intervals until the desired pH value has been reached.
For electronic pH regulation: Open the vent of the CO_2 bottle slightly. Program the desired pH value as the selected value. If the pH value has not been attained after 3 hours, open the vent further. Repeat measurements at 3-hour intervals until the desired value has been reached. After 3 days and then at 6-week intervals, recalibrate the measuring electrode according to the manufacturer's directions.

Step 4: Check the pH value daily at about the same time of day and the carbonate hardness after every water change; if necessary, readjust the CO_2 feed or the carbonate hardness.

• The table cannot be used with peat filtering. Peat filtering falsifies the measurement results because other substances are influencing the pH value besides the CO_2.

• The shaded area on the table shows the CO_2 values that are too high for fish.

• CO_2 values = mg/L.

Determining CO_2 Content in Aquarium Water

pH value ▸ carbonate hardness (°)	6.4	6.6	6.8	7.0	7.2	7.4	7.6	7.8
2°	25	16	10	7	4	3	2	1
4°	50	32	20	13	8	5	3	2
6°	75	50	30	20	12	8	5	3
8°	100	65	40	25	16	10	6	4
10°	130	80	50	32	20	13	8	5
12°	150	100	60	40	24	15	10	6
14°	180	115	70	45	28	18	11	7
16°	200	130	80	50	32	20	12	8
18°	230	145	90	58	36	23	14	9
20°	250	160	100	65	40	25	16	10

Setting up the tank demands care. So that the bottom glass doesn't flex, lay a ¹/₈-in (3-mm)-thick Styrofoam cushion, cut to the size of the glass, under the tank: This keeps small stones, and so on, from producing point stress on the tank floor, which could then break. To provide a firm support for the tank, pet stores offer special stands in which you can also install the external filter and other equipment.

Aquarium tanks are generally supplied with a glass or plastic top and a matching fluorescent light fixture. Covering the tank keeps fish from jumping out of the aquarium and prevents too much water evaporation.

Filtration

Clear, pollutant-free water is achieved with an effective filter.

Every aquarium filter operates by means of two basic principles, which both work simultaneously when the aquarium water is directed through filter material by the pump:

■ The mechanical filter effect "strains" coarse particles of dirt out of the water by means of fine-pored filter material. These are thus removed from the tank, to be sure, but they are still contained in the water circulation of the aquarium. In order to get the strained dirt out of the circulation, the filter material must be cleaned regularly. Cleaning is overdue when the water only runs through the filter very slowly.

■ The biological filtering material makes use of the bacteria that are always present (see page 58). If there are no bacteria (for example, right after a new installation), toxic intermediate products can develop, which can harm the fish. Therefore, you should only put fish into a newly established aquarium after 2 weeks at the earliest. To provide room in the filter for as many bacteria as possible, offer them as large a surface of filter material as possible (see Filter Materials, following). After 2 weeks, enough bacteria will have colonized that a few fish can be put into the tank.

■ Additional filtration can be achieved by using special filter materials. The chemical filter effect depends on the ability of the particular filter material to chemically

Different filter materials:
1 **Foam filter**
2 **Activated carbon**
3 **Siporax rings**
4 **Peat**

alter the aquarium water flowing through it. For instance, by means of a chemical filter effect, you can remove poisons and medications from the aquarium (activated carbon filter) or lower the pH (peat filter).

Filter Types

A filter may be either external or internal, depending on whether it is installed outside the aquarium or inside. Both types can be equipped with mechanical and biologically active filter materials.

In tanks up to 20 gal (76 L), motor- or air-driven molded plastic internal filters (see photo, page 68) have proven effective.

In larger tanks, it is better to use a large external filter (see photo, page 68) or a powerful circulation-pump internal filter.

The intermittent external filter is a version that is especially effective biologically. By a special mechanism, the filter substrate is dried at regular intervals for a short time and provided with air. Thus, the filter bacteria receive more oxygen and work faster. Some external filters, called thermofilters, come with a built-in heating unit, which warms the water flowing through it.

Filter Materials

Plastic sponge has stood the test, especially for internal filters, but also for the uppermost layer in external filters. It is cut to fit, and thus is easy to remove from the aquarium or filter container. Because its pores are coarse, it doesn't clog up with dirt so fast, yet offers enough colonizing area for bacteria. In addition, it lasts for a long time, for which reason it has almost completely replaced the filter pads that used to be commonly employed.

Small ceramic tubes, porous filter gravel, and sintered glass rings (Siporax, see drawing) produce optimal biological filtering in external filters. These filter materials, with their extremely large surface areas, offer bacteria generous space for colonizing.

Activated carbon (see How to Solve Maintenance Problems, page 112) and peat (see Creating Natural Aquariums, page 106) are filter materials with chemical effects. They are best installed in a nylon net bag in external filters.

Carbon Dioxide Fertilizing

Carbon dioxide provides for sturdy plant growth (see page 65). To get amounts of carbon dioxide into the aquarium appropriate for fertilizing plants or lowering pH, you need to understand the relationships between carbonate hardness, pH value, and amount of CO_2 (see table, page 69).

An *optimal* CO_2 *supply* is offered by a CO_2 dosing system (available from the pet store). All models are made the same way, except for the regulating unit.

The CO_2 gas is stored in a pressurized bottle and is directed through pressure-reducing valves by a special hose to the aquarium.

When there are two valves, the second serves to finely adjust the amount of CO_2 admitted. So that the gas dissolves in the aquarium and doesn't immediately evaporate from the surface of the water, a CO_2 reactor sends a stream of small bubbles moving through the aquarium water on the longest pathway possible (see photo, page 68). Depending on the equipment, regulation of the amount introduced is accomplished by hand with the bubble counter or with an electronic regulating unit controlled by the pH value (see Setting Up and Operating a CO_2 System, page 69).

For manually regulated apparatus, an additional night switch to shut off the CO_2 feed is appropriate, because the plants do not need any CO_2 at night.

Heating

Although most of the usual aquarium fish need tropical warmth, very few aquarists know that tropical waters can exhibit very different temperatures. A small forest stream in a tropical region may, for example, be cooler than a sunny marshy pool in the same region. In order to meet the needs of specific fish and plants, a thermostatically controlled aquarium heater is installed to regulate the water temperature. There are three different basic models.

The rod heater consists of a glass-enclosed heating coil and is installed in the aquarium.

With a thermofilter, the heating coil is installed in the external filter container. A temperature sensor is located in the aquarium and is con-

TIP

▼

A constant temperature in the aquarium does not always correspond to natural conditions. Therefore, annually, for example in winter, decrease the temperature by about 4°F (2°C) for about 3 months. In this way, you can imitate the cooler rainy season that occurs in nature. Many fish respond to this with more vitality.

Peacock gobies (*Tateurndina ocellicauda*) are quiet fish for small aquariums.

nected by a wire to the heating unit in the filter (see photo, page 68).

Low-voltage heating cables with transformers and temperature sensors are preferably used when sturdy plant growth is wanted. They are laid on the bottom of the aquarium. There, through the rising warm water, they promote healthy biological activity in the substrate and provide "warm feet" for the water plants.

The wattage of the heater is determined by the temperature fluctuations in the room in which the aquarium is located. If the room is regularly heated during the coldest seasons of the year, you can figure about 2 watts per gal (3.8 L). Only in cold rooms should the heating be increased to 4 watts per gal

(3.8 L). Avoid oversize heaters because in too-small tanks they heat up too fast and produce temperature fluctuations that are too wide.

Lighting

Above all, light is important for sturdy, healthy plant growth.

Recommended are tank covers with integrated light fixtures. To achieve the best light output, make sure that the lights are equipped with reflectors.

Fluorescent lights have proven good for freshwater aquariums, and they are available in different colors. The choice of color is of no importance for normal plant growth.

To achieve the most natural color reflections possible, however, the lamp color "Daylight" is best.

Additional "plant lights," which give off a blue-red light, enhance the colors of bluish iridescent or red fish. However, they should only be used in combination with daylight tubes, because the violet color along looks unnatural.

The amount (intensity) of light is the determining factor for sturdy plant growth. Some-

Can Fish See Colors?

Yes, most fish can see colors. This can be demonstrated during the mating season, especially in the male. They then wear an especially colorful coat of scales. Their colorful display attracts females. An interesting experiment shows that fish see colors. The females of the native stickleback especially like red males to mate with them. The lighting in an aquarium can be so changed that the females can no longer recognize the red males. Now the females can no longer distinguish between red and gray males. They now pair just as often with the gray stickleback males as with the red ones.

one who doesn't care about that and isn't growing any light-loving plants (see page 85) can equip a tank up to 12 in (30 cm) wide and 16 in (40 cm) high with a tank-length fluorescent tube. With wider or higher tanks, you should use two tubes or more. For lush plant growth and plants needing very bright light, with small tanks, you can increase to three or four tubes; for larger ones, up to 28 in (70 cm) wide, increase up to six tubes. Tanks over 24 in (60 cm) high can no longer be effectively lit for plants with fluorescent tubes. Bear in mind that sturdy plant growth also requires more fertilizer.

Oxygen Supply

In a normally populated tank, with a surface moved by the filter outflow, there is no deficit of oxygen, as a rule.

Problems can arise on hot summer days in heavily populated tanks, however. Also, there can be too little oxygen in a well-planted tank at night, because the plants then breathe in more oxygen than they produce.

The remedy is created by aeration with diffusors, small "showers," which are attached to the water outflow of the motorized filter. Alternatively you can use air stones, which are driven by an air pump. Consider, however, that with more aeration and the accompanying movement of the water, you drive out carbon dioxide. Therefore, aeration and CO_2 fertilization don't go together.

To balance the carbon dioxide needs of the plants and the oxygen needs of the fish (and of the plants themselves after the lights are turned off), simulate the natural relationship between plants, fish, and the chemistry of the water they both occupy. For the typical home aquarium, this means having a relatively larger number of plants and a smaller number of fish. With technical equipment, one can make adjustments to achieve the ideal conditions. If one models the aquarium after the natural environment of the fish, the beneficial relationship between plants and fish is achieved almost automatically.

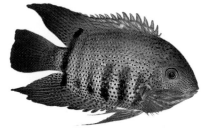

Aquariums Arranged Correctly and Beautifully

Most people think of an aquarium as a "living picture" with an aesthetic and calming effect, achieved by harmonizing your own personal ideas of a beautiful aquarium with the requirements of the fish and the plants.

The Substrate

The substrate fulfills important functions for the fish and the plants in the aquarium: There plants find a foothold and the nutrients they need. The bacteria that break down harmful substances live in it, also. The thickness of the substrate in a planted aquarium should be around $2^1/2$ to 3 in (6 to 8 cm).

Pebbles and Sand

A $2^1/2$- to 3-in (6- to 8-cm) layer of lime-free, smooth, beige quartz pebbles has proved to be best. A grain size of about $1/8$ in (3 to 5 mm) is preferable. You can also use brown lava gravel or black basalt splinters. However, these kinds of pebbles are sharp-edged and must not be used for fish that burrow, such as armored catfish. A thin—about $3/4$ in (2 cm) thick—layer of lime-free

quartz sand is only suitable for tanks in which there are no plants rooting in the bottom. But some fish, for example, *Achirus* or snail cichlids, need it to dig in.

Important: Before putting the substrate material in the aquarium, rinse it in a pail under running water until the water is almost clear.

Slow-release fertilizer bottom: In a planted aquarium, for the bottom layer ($1/2$–$3/4$ in [1–2 cm]) thick, pebbles that are mixed with slow-release fertilizer (not widely available) especially for water plants are used. Do not wash these pebbles!

The Background

Background plastic made to look natural (see photo, page 78), gives the impression of a natural bank in the aquarium.

This must be carefully attached to the aquarium by the appropriate means for the material (please follow the package directions). For external backgrounds, there are ones printed with underwater motifs or color patterns (see photo, page 78) that can be attached with cellophane tape.

Macrognathus aculeatus
should be provided with lots of
hiding places in the aquarium.

Timetable for Setting Up

Follow the step-by-step plan on these double-spread pages to set up an aquarium:

1 Place the glass tank on a Styrofoam pad. Make sure that the floor and the stand can support the weight (see page 66).

2 Install all technical equipment (filter, heater, carbon dioxide doser, any measuring instruments) without starting it up (see photo 1). Follow the instructions for installing.

3 If you want to attach a background inside, install it now, as well as any bottom heating (see photo 2). You may have to adjust the position of some of the equipment parts in the aquarium until you achieve the best possible function.

4 If you plan to introduce large piles of rock, put a thin Styrofoam underlayer on the aquarium floor, but only where the big rocks are going to lie. Then put in the pile and remove any superfluous bits of Styrofoam, because they will float up when water is added.

5 In an aquarium that is to be planted, put in a layer of pebbles with slow-release fertilizer (not widely available)

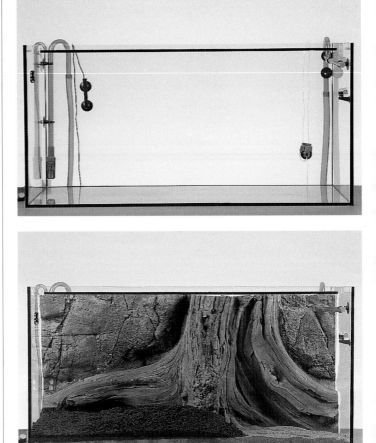

about ³/4 in (2 cm) thick and smooth it with your hand. On top of that comes a pebble layer 1¹/2 to 2¹/2 in (4 to 6 cm) thick.

Photo 1: Install technical equipment.
Photo 2: Add background, undergravel heating, slow-release fertilizer, and gravel.

Photo 3: Add driftwood and rocks; fill one-third full of water; add plants.
Photo 4: Fill with water.

driftwood at first with cotton thread. Then carefully add enough temperature water to fill the aquarium to one-third (pay attention to water values!). Let the stream of water run onto the gravel over a small dish. This keeps the gravel from being stirred up (see photo 3).

7 Now put in the remaining plants, fill the aquarium with temperate water, and start up the technical equipment. At first, the water will be a little cloudy. Put in the water preparation additives from the pet store. Now install the lighting (see photo 4).

8 Let the aquarium run for at least two weeks until the bacteria are established in the aquarium and the plants are growing. Regulate the equipment as necessary. Cloudy water will clarify in the course of this period.

9 Only buy the fish when the two weeks have passed and the water has become clear (see Tips for Buying and Adding the Fish, page 82).

10 Rather than adding all the fish at once, purchase a few, wait a week or two, and add a few more. It is a wise practice to perform a partial water change before each introduction of new fish.

6 Now add small stones and driftwood. If you are working with attached plants (see page 82), these must be fastened to the stones and

A 47-inch (120-cm) tank with many rooted plants and bleeding heart tetras.

Materials for Decoration

Different decorating materials are used to structure the space in the aquarium attractively, offer the fish hiding places, and provide bases for attached plants:

Driftwood, available from the pet store, creates a "comfortable" environment for fish that love its shelter for hiding places. Let the driftwood soak for several days in a large container to leach out most of the acidifying substances and so that it will absorb as much water as possible. Because of its acidifying effect, driftwood is not suitable for fish that need alkaline water.

Stones and rock piles are best made of sandstone, shale, lava, granite, and basalt. Make sure that the rock contains no lime, which hardens the water.

Take care to set the rocks so they can't tip over.

Pottery caves and tubes are gladly taken over for hiding places by many fish. Soak the pottery caves in a pail for at least a day.

©*Takashi Amano, Aqua Design Amano Co., Ltd.*

Tips for Buying and Adding the Fish

■ Inform yourself, before buying, about the needs of the species that you want to keep (see descriptions section, beginning on page 14).
■ Choose fish species whose needs you can satisfy in your aquarium.
■ Only buy fish when your aquarium is established (see pages 78–79).
■ Check out the healthiness of the fish in the pet dealer's tanks (see table, page 95).
■ Transport the warmly packed fish home the fastest way.
■ Equalize the water temperature in the fish bag with that of the aquarium. To do so, allow the bag to float on the upper surface of the water in the aquarium for at least 30 minutes.
■ Now open the bag and let some aquarium water run into it.
■ Wait another 10 minutes before you let the fish into the tank.

Various Types of Water Plants

Attached plants don't grow in the ground but on stones or roots. They take their nutrients from the water. Planting and care tip: Fasten them to the particular decorative object with a cotton thread. Later, by the time the thread has rotted, they will be attached on their own. Cut back moss cushions now and again or remove leaves.

Rosette plants put forth leaves from a single leaf rosette at the transition to the roots. They are rooted deep in the bottom substrate and draw the major portion of their nutrients from it. Depending on their size (see table, page 85), they are good for either foreground or background plantings. Planting and care tip: Carefully free the roots from any rock wool that may be wrapped around them and cut them back with scissors to about 1¹/₂ in (4 cm). Plant

Water plants:
1 African water fern (*Bolbitis heudelotii*)
2 Java fern (*Microsorium pteropus*)
3 *Rotala*
4 Amazon sword plant (*Echinodorus parviflorus*)

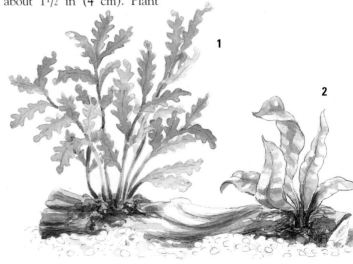

them in a small hole that you have bored into the substrate with a finger, making sure not to bury the crown. Remove old leaves now and then.

Bunch plants form scarcely any roots, so some of them can also be cultivated as floating plants (e.g., horn-wort, *Naiad* species, broad-leaved Indian fern). They need more light than rosette plants. Planting and care tip: Cut a little off the stems at the bottom and carefully press about three stems at once into the ground. If they float up, anchor with plant lead. To keep bunch plants bushy and the growth young, cut off the tips when they have reached the water surface.

Floating plants shade the underlayers of water and are very much beloved by fish who live under the water surface and seek cover there. Floating plants tolerate no current. Care tip: Thin the growth often.

Care of Water Plants

The substrate in any aquarium becomes compacted over time, and this results in an unfavorable condition for plants. Therefore, don't use sand but only lime-poor gravel with a grain size of about $1/8$ in (2 to 5 mm). The nutrient supply is provided at installation with slow-release fertilizer (see page 76). Maintain good substrate condition over the long term by periodically "vacuuming" the substrate with a siphon made for this purpose, as part of the routine water change procedure (see page 86).

Light, carbon dioxide (CO_2), carbonate hardness, pH value, and water temperature are also important maintenance factors. In regard to this, read Water, the Life Element (pages 58 to 65) and Technical Equipment—A Must for the Aquarium (pages 66 to 75).

3

4

Note: For most plants, the best conditions are a pH value of around 7 and 3 to 12 dKH.

Provision of nutrients with salts and trace elements is guaranteed by regular additions of special water plant fertilizers. Because the essential iron cannot be combined in a bottle with these fertilizers, you must buy an extra fertilizer to provide iron. Fertilize after each water change but in moderation. The need for fertilizer depends on the growth habit of the plants. If they grow slowly, they need less fertilizer, and vice versa. Because the package instructions for the fertilizer are oriented toward vigorous plant growth, start with half the quantity recommended. You should not fertilize at all during the first 2 weeks after setting up the aquarium, when the plants have not started growing yet. Later, you can increase the amount with each water change until you think the plant growth is optimal, provided that the other maintenance factors are also optimal.

The table at the right lists water plant species that are satisfied with average water, nutrient, and light values: dKH 3 to 12, pH up to 7.5, 15–20 mg/L CO_2, two tank-length fluorescent light tubes with up to 20 in (50 cm) in tank width and height. Species that can also tolerate harder water are marked with an asterisk (*).

1 Fanwort (*Cabomba caroliniana*) (see photo, page 123)
2 Corkscrew eelgrass (*Vallisneria spiralis*)
3 *Cryptocoryne affinis*
4 Broad-leaved Indian fern (*Ceratopteris thalictroides*)

Easy-to-Care-for Aquarium Plants

English Name	Latin Name	Type	Height in (cm)	Temperature °F (°C)
None	*Anubias barteri* var. *nana*	Attached	2–6 (5–15)	72–82 (22–28)
Java fern	*Microsorium pteropus*	Attached	6–12 (15–30)	68–82 (20–28)
Java moss	*Vesicularia dubyana*	Attached	moss	59–86 (15–30)
African water fern	*Bolbitis heudelotii*	Attached	8–20 (20–50)	72–79 (22–26)
None	*Cryptocoryne affinis**	Rosette	4–16 (10–40)	72–79 (22–26)
None	*Cryptocoryne aponogetifolia**	Rosette	up to 39 (100)	70–81 (21–27)
None	*Cryptocoryne beckettii**	Rosette	4–10 (10–25)	72–79 (22–26)
Slender-leaved Amazon sword plant	*Echinodorus amazonicus*	Rosette	12–20 (30–50)	72–79 (22–26)
Broad-leaved Amazon sword plant	*Echinodorus bleheri*	Rosette	16–24 (40–60)	72–82 (22–28)
Amazon sword plant	*Echinodorus osiris*	Rosette	16–24 (40–60)	64–79 (18–26)
Amazon sword plant	*Echinodorus parviflorus*	Rosette	8–16 (20–40)	72–75 (22–24)
Pygmy chain sword	*Echinodorus tenellus*	Rosette	up to 2 (5)	64–82 (18–28)
Hairgrass	*Eleocharis acicularis*	Rosette	8–20 (20–50)	72–77 (22–25)
Dwarf arrowhead	*Sagittaria subulata**	Rosette	4–24 (10–60)	64–82 (18–28)
Eelgrass	*Vallisneria americana**	Rosette	over 39 (100)	72–79 (22–26)
Corkscrew eelgrass	*Vallisneria spiralis**	Rosette	12–20 (30–50)	68–82 (20–28)
Hornwort	*Ceratophyllum demersum**	Floating	———	64–86 (18–30)
None	*Najas guadelupensis*	Floating	———	68–86 (20–30)
Crystalwort	*Riccia fluitans*	Floating	———	68–81 (20–27)
None	*Bacopa monnieri*	Stem	———	64–82 (18–28)
Broad-leaved Indian fern	*Ceratopteris thalictroides**	Stem	———	72–82 (22–28)
Indian water star	*Hygrophila difformis**	Stem	———	75–82 (24–28)
None	*Hygrophila corymbosa**	Stem	———	75–82 (24–28)
Indian water friend	*Hygrophila polysperma**	Stem	———	72–82 (22–28)

Aquarium Maintenance Made Easy

The total maintenance requirement for an optimally designed aquarium is astonishingly small if you undertake a water change once a week.

Maintenance Equipment
- Two buckets (3 to 5 gal (11 to 19 L), which are used exclusively for aquarium purposes
- A hose 8 ft (2.4 m) long 1/2 in (12 to 16 mm) in diameter with a bottom vacuuming funnel from the pet store
- A glass scraper to remove algae (e.g., algae magnet)
- One large and one small aquarium fishnet

Weekly Partial Water Change
By doing a regular weekly water change of 25 to 30 percent of the aquarium water volume, you accomplish several things:
- You remove toxic substances that have accumulated during the week, especially nitrates, which even a good filter cannot take care of.
- You remove food remnants and other decaying organic matter before it is converted to toxic material if you "vacuum" the bottom with a siphon designed for this purpose.

- You reintroduce trace elements, which are present in the tap water. During the week, these are used up by the plants and animals.
- You stimulate the vitality of your fish with fresh water.

How to Make a Partial Water Change
Disconnect all equipment. Then, with a hose that is provided at one end with a modified funnel, you siphon out the water into a large bucket. Take out as many pailsful of aquarium water as necessary for 25 to 30 percent of the tank volume to be removed. Using the same hose, refill the aquarium again with temperature-adjusted and, if necessary, re-treated water.

Don't forget to put in the plant fertilizer if you have a planted tank. Reconnect the equipment.

Carrying out some additional procedures during the weekly water change will save work later:
- Remove algae from the front and side glass with the algae magnet. If you don't do this weekly, the dot-shaped, hard-to-remove algae will colonize more readily.
- Carefully loosen the substrate with an implement

TIP

Dry food is a good basis for your fish's diet. However, the food spoils very quickly once the bottle is opened. Therefore, reclose the bottle carefully after every use so that the flakes don't absorb the humidity and begin to get moldy.

Three-spot gourami (*Trichogaster trichopterus*) do not have any demanding water-quality requirements.

such as a fork. The bottom stays porous longer and you will have flourishing plants.

■ Clean the cover. It gets calcium deposits very quickly and is then much harder to clean.

■ In an external filter, rinse the topmost layer of the filter substrate under warm but not hot water; in an internal filter, rinse the foam cartridge (topmost). This removes much dirt from the water circulation and it then is not broken down into pollutants. The biological filter remains active.

Maintenance Timetable

■ Observe your fish daily for several minutes while feeding. Thus you can discover early signs of illness (see table, page 95) or possible clues to faulty maintenance (see How to Solve Maintenance Problems, beginning on page 112).

■ Check daily to see if the filter discharge has slowed, the pH value (permanent pH meter) is in the optimal range, the carbon dioxide doser is functioning (check bubble counter), and the temperature is correct.

■ At irregular intervals, you should clean the pump head of your circulating pump filter

according to the manufacturer's instructions, cut back the plants, and every 6 weeks clean and calibrate the probe on the electronic pH meter if used.

■ Stock up on food supplies in advance. Change fluorescent bulbs yearly if you want intensive plant growth.

The Right Diet

With different types of food available at the pet store, you can feed almost all fish species a balanced and varied diet.

Proper fish maintenance includes taking into consideration the dietary ingredients that the particular fish in question enjoy in nature.

Therefore, not every type of food is suitable for all fish equally.

Dry food varieties by reputable manufacturers offer a basic diet that is of high value qualitatively but is very rich for most fish species. Therefore, make sure to alternate dry foods with other types of food. Always feed dry food with a roughage-rich green element (best from spirulina algae).

You can get dry food as flakes, granules, and tablets. Flakes are good for all free-

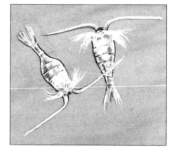

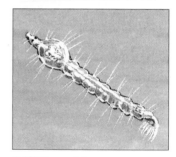

1 Cyclops

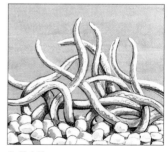

2 White gnat larvae

3 Tubifex

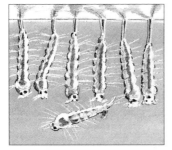

4 Black gnat larvae

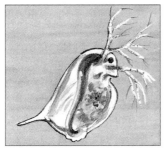

5 Water flea

6 Red gnat larvae

swimming fish; tablets sink to reach bottom-dwelling fish. Granules (or the larger pellets) are suitable for cichlids.

Microcrustaceans of different species are offered by the dealer frozen or, depending on the time of year, live (see drawings 1 and 5). Their roughage content is higher than that of dry food and should be alternated with it. Also, larger fish enjoy the small cyclops (*Cyclops*). Water fleas (*Daphnia, Bosmina*) have the greatest roughage content and are not suitable for any fish species as the sole feed. Frozen *Mysis* shrimps and adult *Artemia* brine shrimp replace the little cyclops and water fleas for the larger fish. The small live-food specialists and fry, which eat only live food, can regularly be provided with *Artemia* nauplii (baby *Artemia*). The breeding of *Artemia* nauplii is described under the heading Food for Fry (see page 90).

Gnat (bloodworms) or mosquito *larvae*, frozen or live, as an alternative to larger organisms provide variety (see drawings 2, 4, and 6).

White gnat larvae are given to larger fish, black to smaller fish. Insect-eating fish will often take only black gnat larvae as the single alternative. Red gnat larvae (bloodworms) should never be fed because of the possibility of contamination with pesticides.

Live *Tubifex* worms (from the pet store) are very rich. They should only be fed now and then (see drawing 3). Let the worms soak in a small pail for several days before feeding. Change the water in the pail several times daily.

Insects are an important food for many surface fish, especially for killifish. The smallest and most commonly fed insect is the fruit fly *Drosophila*. If you are interested in killifish, provide yourself with a breeding kit from the pet store, which also carries larger insects, such as crickets and mealworms, which freshwater butterfly fish enjoy.

Put the insects in the refrigerator for awhile before feeding so that they are slowed and don't escape while being fed.

Green food is absolutely a daily necessity for many mailed catfish but also for other fish. You can try the various kinds from the supermarket (carefully washed), for example, blanched lettuce, cucumber slices, slices of red potato, mashed peas.

Place the food so that the catfish find it on the bottom and that the next day you can just quickly remove any rotting leftovers from the aquarium.

Vitamins as additional food supplements are unnecessary if you follow the feeding rules (see page 91). Furthermore, it is difficult to dissolve vitamins, which are mostly fat-soluble, with the food in the aquarium water.

Food for Fry

Fry need small food and must be fed several times a day during their growing phase.

Live *Artemia* nauplii can be bred from preserved eggs at home: Fill one 1-qt (1-L) canning jar with 1 qt (1 L) of saltwater made from 4 tsp (20 g) of uniodized table salt and 1 qt (1 L) of water. Add 1/4 tsp of *Artemia* eggs from the pet store. Aerate the culture with an air stone. At 75–82°F (24–28°C) (put jars in a water bath with an aquarium heater), the reddish larvae hatch out. With a feeding syringe or a pipette, suck up only the larvae near

the bottom. Strain the larvae (using an *Artemia* net from the pet store), rinse briefly with tap water, and feed immediately. Start a new culture every day in order to always have enough larvae.

Dry food for fry should never, ever be used as supplementary food in an established aquarium. It is very fine and disperses too fast in a large aquarium, and then the water becomes loaded up with it.

In a special rearing tank with no bottom substrate, on the other hand, it can be used with care if the bottom is regularly vacuumed with a thin hose.

Food tablets are a rich food that should only be fed sparingly.

Can Fish Overeat?

Yes, fish can overeat. In the wild, the food is usually scanty. The fish are therefore conditioned to eat everything that is available to them for food. If the food you put into the aquarium is too much, they will nevertheless eat it all up.

The fish act in the aquarium just as they are used to doing in the wild. There are fish that so overeat, they die right away. Others, however, die slowly of obesity.

Feeding Rules

1 Feed once a day and only as much as the fish can eat in 2 minutes.

Fish have no "brakes on eating" and can easily eat more than they can digest. Many aquarium fish are therefore overweight. An exception is green food, which should be "presented" for an entire day.

2 Feed different kinds of food on different days: Dry food provides a good foundation but it is too rich in protein to be fed every day all by itself.

Alternate with live food, for example, or various frozen foods, because they have a lower percentage of protein.

3 Mammal proteins, such as beef, are hard for fish to digest and lead to liver problems. Therefore, don't give them any foods containing beef.

4 *Tubifex* and red gnat larvae are usually contaminated. Thirty percent of humans have an allergic reaction to red gnat larvae. Therefore, only feed rinsed *Tubifex* and don't feed any red gnat larvae at all.

5 Make one day a week a fast day for your fish.

6 Take into consideration the special food requirements (type of food, time of day for feeding) of all species in the aquarium.

7 Buy foods in small quantities that will be used up quickly; for example, within one month. In this way, you help ensure that the food is fresh and provides the maximum nutritional value. If dry food becomes moldy or develops an odor of spoilage, discard it immediately. Keep frozen foods solidly frozen, thawing out only as much as required for a single feeding.

Most people are aware of the health benefits they derive from eating a wholesome, well-balanced diet. It is suprising that many do not realize that fish need an appropriate diet for all the same reasons that people do. In the streams and lakes where our aquarium fish make their natural homes, the most abundant and heavily foraged foods—crustaceans, insects, worms, and algae, are all alive and fresh. Professional fish breeders for years recognized the benefits of live foods.

Treating Illnesses

Normally your fish will remain healthy with proper maintenance because their resistance is strong. Most diseases, unfortunately, arise from faulty maintanence.

Maintenance Faults

Check first to see if:

■ the nitrate values are too high;

■ there are dead fish in the aquarium;

■ the water quality is the right one for the fish;

■ the food is correct for the fish;

■ there is enough aeration;

■ the filter is working;

■ the last water change was put off for too long;

■ the tank is too crowded;

■ aggressive fish are chasing the others and keeping them from eating.

If any of these conditions is present, repair the fault as quickly as possible.

Poisoning as a Cause of Illness

Poisoning from tainted tap water, wrong medication or overdosage, or faulty care occurs more often then infectious diseases. You can recognize poisoining of the fish by the following symptoms,

which can appear alone or in combination:

■ Breathing problems ("hanging" under the water surface)

■ Extreme fearfulness

■ Dashing around in the tank

■ Noticeable pallor or extremely intense color

■ Tumbling movements

■ Apathy

Immediate measures include carefully changing 90 percent of the aquarium water for tap water into which you have mixed a dechlorinator from the pet store (watch the temperature!). In addition, filter over activated carbon (from the pet store; follow directions on the package). If the symptoms decrease, stop the activated carbon after 2 weeks and do another partial water change (see page 86).

Note: Tap water poisoning can be caused by copper (from copper water piping) or too high a chlorine content ("swimming pool smell"). Remove chlorine with vigorous aeration of water in a bucket or by letting it stand for 2 days. Dechlorinating agents can do the job instantly.

You must not use water from copper piping as aquarium water anymore.

Veil-tailed guppies (*Poecilia reticulata* var.) come in many different color patterns.

Infectious Diseases

A *table salt bath* helps for fungus infections, *Ichthyophthirius*, mild attacks of skin and gill flukes. Treatment is carried out in a pail.

Administration: 2–3 tsp (10–15 g) table salt per 1 qt (1 L) water. Let fish swim in it for 20 minutes under observation.

Important: With *Ichthyophthirius*, all fish must be treated, without exception. After the first treatment, repeat the bath two more times at intervals of 48 to 72 hours.

A *Formalin dip* helps for skin and gill flukes and many other external parasites. The treatment is carried out in a pail.

Administration: Put 0.07–0.14 fl oz (2–4 mL) Formalin (35 to 40 percent solution) in 10 qt (10 L) of water. Bathe the fish in the solution for 30 minutes at the most. With any sign of disturbances in balance, immediately put the fish back in the maintenance tank.

Caution: Formalin is a strong corrosive. Do not let it get in contact with skin, eyes, or mucous membranes. Be certain to keep it out of the reach of children!

A *warm treatment* helps with mild attacks of *Ichthyophthirius*, *Oodinium*, and other external parasites. The treatment is carried out in the maintenance tank.

Administration: Only in tanks with clean water and good oxygen supply. Raise the temperature by 2°F (1°C) per hour. At any signs of reaction in the fish, such as disturbances in balance, discontinue the therapy.

Note: Disinfect fishnets that have come in contact with sick fish for 3 days, with a net disinfectant solution sold in pet stores. Afterward, carefully rinse out the nets. This way, you will avoid new infection.

It is worth remembering that the most common problem, infestation by the external parasite *Ichthyophthirius*, often develops as a result of stressful conditions. For example, failure of a heater could result in an overnight drop in water temperature, or inadequate maintenance could result in the accumulation of waste products in the water. These situations create stress for the fish, lowering their resistance to infestation by the microscopic parasites.

1 Hole-in-the-head disease

2 White spot

3 Velvet disease

Recognizing and Treating Illnesses

Symptoms	Diagnosis	Therapy
White spots, up to ¹/₂ in (1.5 cm) in size, on the upper surface of the body; possibly labored breathing; rubbing against objects.	**White spot** (*Ichthyophthirius*) (see drawing 2)	Warmth treatment (10 days at 86°F [30°C]), table salt bath, or medications containing malachite green oxalate.
Small dots, up to 0.3 mm in size—often thick as a whitish or yellowish deposit; possibly labored breathing; rubbing against objects.	**Velvet disease** (*Oodinium*) (see drawing 3)	Warmth treatments (24 to 36 hours at 91–93°F [33–34°C]).
Tattered fins, often shortened, with or without a white edge.	**Bacterial fin rot**	Medications containing furazolidone.
Small holes in the head region, becoming larger with time, often covered with a white coating; dark coloration of the body; white, stringy, slimy feces.	**Hole-in-the-head disease** (see drawing 1)	For mild attack: feed vitamin-rich diet; for more severe attack (stringy feces), ask the veterinarian for Gabrocol or metronidazole (Clont).
Vigorous swallowing movements and/or prominent gill covers; labored breathing; rubbing against objects.	**Gill/skin flukes**	Formalin bath, table salt bath.
Swollen body, often with projecting scales; bulging eyes.	**Dropsy**	Medications containing furazolidone. *Note:* Medications containing malachite green oxalate and furazolidone are available at the pet store.

Understand, learn, and observe

In natural aquariums fish show entire range of their fascinating behavior. You'll learn by watching them.

Correctly Interpreting Behavior Patterns

Often you may observe fish behavior that is difficult to understand at first. Thus, this chapter presents examples of behavior you can observe in your aquarium and what it tells you about your fish.

Fish Are Interesting Creatures

Fish are unfairly said to be boring. Anyone who has observed the fish community in an aquarium that is correctly arranged for the species for any length of time is impressed by the variety of their behaviors. Thus, between two snail cichlid males there often occurs exciting looking but harmless mouth fighting. A puffer sneaks up in a fascinating way on his chief prey, a snail (see photograph, page 100).

Also, many fish parents, such as labyrinth fish or cichlids, go about raising their offspring with a devotion that you might only have attributed to the more highly developed mammals (see photograph, page 104).

Schooling Behavior

Most fish spend at least a part of their lives with others of their species, sometimes even with companions of other species, together in a school. Even many cichlids, which at least during mating aggressively defend a territory, in their youth behave like characins in a school.

In most instances, the reason for forming a school is the double protection effect:

■ For one thing, predators that are after one animal have difficulty concentrating on the individual animal among numbers of fish.

■ For the other, for the members of the school, there is a "diluting effect." When a predator has focused on a single prey animal, the probability that it can catch that particular one among the many others of the species is less. The risk of becoming a victim is, thus, less for any individual when it swims with the others in a school.

School formation can be observed in the aquarium, particularly when the fish perceive danger ahead. The formation of a school is particularly easy to observe when you have released several new animals into the aquarium. Like the rainbow fish in the photograph on

TIP

Often behavior patterns cannot be understood immediately when you observe them. Note in a fish journal all the striking behavior patterns and compare them later. Perhaps later you will recognize the connection to the behavior of the fish.

Apistogramma cacatuoides **males. These two are displaying for each other with fins spread.**

pages 62–63, as first they draw together uncertainly.

The cardinal tetras in the photograph on pages 102–103, on the other hand, have already gotten acclimated and have spread out over almost the entire tank.

Territorial Behavior and Fighting

Many fish, including many so-called school fish, form territories at least temporarily, and they defend them against fish of the same species or fish of other species with more or less vigorous fighting. *The basis for forming territories is* always the defense of something that the individual fish can lose in competition: a good place with plenty of food (feeding territory), an environment that is especially suitable for raising young (brooding territory), or the best place to court passing females (courting territory).

Territory building in the aquarium can be observed, particularly with cichlids.

The mbuna (see photograph, page 110), who eat their offspring, not only defend their feeding territory in their native habitat, Lake Malawi, but also in the aquar-

Some puffers (*Carinotetraodon lorteti*) sneak up on their chief pray, the water snail, with scarcely perceptible movements.

ium. Even if there are no algae growing in the aquarium, they do not give up their natural behavior pattern.

The female ram, on the other hand, defends a "portable" brood-care territory, namely the leaf on which she has laid her eggs (see photograph, page 104).

In danger, a larger cichlid might take the leaf stem in its mouth and pull it into more secure shallow water.

Problems with territory building and fighting in the aquarium always arise when the territory claimed is the size of the entire aquarium. Other fish are then aggressively chased by the territory owner because he intends to

How Does the Neon Tetra Light Up?

In the aquarium, you can see that the neon tetras light up. They have very fine luminescent particles in their blue luminous stripes on both sides. Even very little light is reflected by these luminescent particles—rather like the reflecting strips on your school bag.

In the wild, neon tetras live in dark primeval forest streams. The light stripes help them keep in contact with their school. At night, when the neon tetras sleep, they position their light stripes so that they no longer reflect any light. In this way, they avoid the possibility that in moonlight, for example, a predatory fish may discover them while they are sleeping and devour them.

"defend" his territory, but they cannot flee. In this case, you must either take the territory owner or the other fish out of the aquarium. An emergency solution for such cases appears on page 116.

Reproductive Behavior

The most exciting things to watch are the sometimes adventurous efforts that some fish undertake to bring their offspring securely into the next fish generation.

Species Without Brood Care

Some fish species, like many characins, barbs, and rainbow fish, let breeding occur with little expenditure of effort: They lay their eggs after a brief courtship in a more or less protected place and leave them to their fate. The females of the live-bearing species don't bother about their offspring after the birth of the fry. Often, the fry must even be protected from the cannibalistic lusts of their mother. On the other hand, other fish form proper families until the fry are over the worst. At least among the brood-raising species, there is a single parent father or mother who takes care of the young.

Fish with a Sense of Family

Among the most attentive of all the fish parents are certainly the pair-forming cichlids. Some species, such as the angelfish, court with trembling movements, often for several weeks, before they decide to "bond for life." When both partners have finally agreed to found a family together, they often inspect several places for spawning before they actually deposit eggs in one of them (see photograph, pages 96–97).

For several weeks, the father and mother care for the young until they are about 1 in (2 cm) long.

With many mouthbrooding cichlids, for instance, all Malawi cichlids, the mother exclusively cares for the young.

To provide security for her offspring in the first weeks of their life, she takes the eggs in her mouth right after they are spawned, broods them there, and only lets the fry out when they are fully developed miniature editions of the mother.

This aquarium is arranged in a Japanese style and is occupied by cardinal tetras.

Some species swim back into the mother's mouth at night or when in danger during the first few days.

Also with mouthbrooders, there are species in which both sexes take care of the young, for example, the *Chromidotilapia finleyi*.

Species with male brood care are found in the labyrinth fish and its relatives, which are fascinating because they build bubble nests. Here the female makes herself scarce when she has laid her eggs in the nest that the male has artfully constructed in one day.

The male, such as the lace gourami male, cares for the eggs and the larvae until they swim freely and have spread throughout the weed thickets.

A Cuckoo in the Aquarium

Nature has produced something quite special with the cuckoo catfish (*Synodontis multipunctatus*), which is easy to maintain in an aquarium.

The catfish parents do not themselves take care of the fry but seek out an (involuntary) nursemaid for their offspring. The bird cuckoos do the same thing. When catfish that are ready to spawn have found a spawning pair of mouthbrooding cichlids, they shove their own eggs underneath the cichlid's in a lightning spawning action. This action is then completed at the moment the cichlids have finished their own spawning and take them in their mouth to brood them.

The catfish fry then hatch in the cichlid's mouth and help themselves to a simple food supply: the eggs and larvae in the mouth of the cichlid.

Intentional Breeding of Aquarium Fish

Reproduction in the aquarium often runs into difficulties

so that usually a separate aquarium is set up for breeding. Only, thus, can the potential parents be kept free from disturbances or can the special water conditions be created that the fish need to get into the mood for mating.

In underpopulated aquariums, however, it is still possible to raise some fish of

The female ram, or butterfly dwarf cichlid (*Microgeophagus ramirezi*), tends her spawn on a leaf.

TIP

Dried beech and oak leaves are good for creating a natural substrate for the aquarium bottom. But you should only use leaves that you have collected during the winter from the branches and not fallen leaves. Thus, you will avoid introducing fungus spores into the aquarium and forming a dense, toxic carpet of fungus strands on the leaves.

brood-caring and live-bearing species. Primarily, you need to pay attention to two things:

■ Creating enough hiding places, depending on the fish species, for example, in the form of dense plant growth or holes in piles of stones.

■ Providing for additional feedings for the fry, for example *Artemia* nauplii (see Food for Fry, page 90).

In a brooding tank, there is naturally a greater chance of raising the fry. Carefully dip the fry out of the maintenance tank, for instance, with a drinking glass. The sensitive young fish absolutely must stay underwater.

The brooding tank has no bottom substrate. Thus, fish food can be siphoned out with a thin hose more easily.

A small, air-driven internal filter as well as some snails to eat up the food leftovers complete the equipment.

In addition, Java moss creates hiding places for the fry.

Feed the fry two to three times a day. Change one-third of the aquarium water in the brooding tank daily. Siphon off the floor of the tank daily!

If you do all these things, your young fish will thrive splendidly.

Note: Anyone who wants to try breeding aquarium fish will not lack for special literature (see Useful Addresses and Literature, page 125).

As the fry grow, it will become necessary to transfer them to larger, or additional, aquariums for "growing out." The fry will grow more quickly if they are not crowded, and the lower population density will make it easier to maintain proper water conditions in the aquarium. Observe the young fish carefully for abnormalities; a small percentage of any batch almost always exhibits deformities or poor coloration. Any unhealthy individuals should be removed and euthanized.

Creating Natural Aquariums

You can experience a "small natural wonder" in your home if, when installing and stocking your aquarium, you work toward a natural look, that is, establish a "natural" aquarium.

Imitating Nature

In their native habitats, all tropical fish are a part of the total, often fantastically diverse, natural world. Each fish lives there in its "own" special environment in brooks, rivers, swamps, lakes, and ponds.

This chapter contains some suggestions for biotope aquariums. First, the environmental character of the biotope is detailed in short individual descriptions. For stocking the aquarium, only fish species described elsewhere in this book have been considered. But because for many environments not all the fish are imported and so are not available, it has been impossible to avoid using some "foreign" fish in the sugges-

Clear, still water with water lilies at the edge of a flowing stream.

The *Rasbora maculata* lives mostly in the blackwater of Southeast Asia.

tions (e.g., algae-eating fish). Concerning the water values and temperature, go by the water types that are suitable for the particular fish species (see profiles, from page 14).

Clear Water Rain Forest Brook in Hill Country

(See photograph, page 109.)

Biotope character: Fast-flowing, often sunny brooks with clear water. Fine gravel streambeds, in which long-leaved plants find a foothold. Round, algae-covered stones offer fish protection from too strong a current. Old wood collects in deeper places.

Aquarium arrangement: A sturdy filter in a shallow tank provides current. Only in the vicinity of the filter

discharge, where long-leaved plants (e.g., *Cryptocoryne aponogetifolia*) root and partly shade the tank with their flowing leaves, is there slow-release fertilizer under the layer of gravel, which is a mere 1¹/₂ in (4 cm) thick.

Put some round stones and some driftwood in the tank.

Put stone caves in aquariums with cichlids.

Tank size: 39 × 16 × 16 in (100 × 40 × 40 cm); light with two fluorescent light tubes.

Fish suggestions: **West Africa:** 1 pair of *Chromidotilapia finleyi*. A school (12) of Nigerian lamp-eyes; for algae control, 3 *Crossocheilus siamensis* from Asia. **Central America:** 1 pair of convict or firemouth cichlids, 6 to 8 swordtails; for control of algae, 1 pair of *Ancistrus*. **Southeast Asia:** A large school (20–30) of zebra danios, 5 *Crossocheilus siamensis* (Siamese algae-eater). **Australia/Sulawesi:** 12 *Pseudomugil furcatus* or 8 Celebes rainbow fish, 6 halfbeaks; 5 *Crossocheilus siamensis*.

Clear Water Lowland Rain Forest Brook

(See photograph, page 60.)

Biotope character: Shaded, slow-flowing brooks with

sandy or fine-graveled substrates. A layer of dead leaves on the pool bottom offers protection to small fish. Various water plants thrive where the sun pierces the canopy of rain forest trees.

Aquarium arrangement: Substrate $2^1/2$-in (6-cm) thick with slow-release fertilizer for good growth of shadow-loving rosette plants (e.g., cryptocorynes). Driftwood is clustered densely at the back of the tank as if it were washed up there by natural means. The driftwood is planted on the upper sides with attached plants. Along the edges of the aquarium and between the branches, moderately tall cryptocorynes are planted. In front of the driftwood, dead leaves with a hard structure (e.g., red beech, oak) are lying on the ground.

Tank size: 32 × 14 × 16 in (80 × 35 × 40 cm); illuminate with one fluorescent tube.

Suggestions for fish: **West Africa:** 1 pair of dwarf cichlids (*Pelvicachromis* species) or 3 pairs of steel-blue killies, 5 orange-throated panchax, 6 Nigerian lamp-eyes. **South America:** 1 trio (1 male, 2 females) of *Apistogramma cacatuoides* or 6 armored cat-

fish; 8 rosy-finned tetras, 1 pair of whiptails.

Black Water Rain Forest Brook

(See photograph, page 8.)

Biotope character: Slow-flowing lowland brooks on fine, white sand beds. Blackwater is darkly colored but clear, because it contains no matter in suspension. The dark color is caused by incompletely broken-down plant acids (humic acid and others), which give the soft water a pH value of under 6. (Almost) no plants will grow anymore in this nutrient-poor water. A dense layer of leaves covers the bottom in still places. In

Nanochromis transvestitus comes from the blackwater of Zaire.

TIP

▼

You are maintaining your fish correctly for their species if you duplicate a piece of their natural habitat in the aquarium. Even if this piece is tiny and incomplete compared to the natural environment, your charges feel their best in a natural aquarium.

Many swiftly flowing mountain streams are extremely clear, like this West African brook covered with water lilies.

places with stronger current, there are pieces of wood lying directly on the white sand.

Aquarium arrangement: The tank without plants achieves its own special character by means of peat-filtered, very soft, and therefore red-brown water. The background is a layer of small driftwood; in the foreground, the sand substrate, only 1 in (3 cm) thick, is covered with a thin layer of dead leaves

(e.g., red beech, oak). At places with more current, you see the white sand.

Note on water care: The extreme water values (water type 1, see page 14) for blackwater fish must only be reproduced for the species listed below; other fish cannot tolerate them. Regular water change with softened water is important because with the extreme water values, the effectiveness of biological filtering is limited.

Tank size: 39 × 16 × 16 in (100 × 40 × 40 cm); illuminate with one fluorescent tube.

Suggestions for fish: **Indonesia:** 1 pair of lace gouramis, 25 *Rasbora hengeli* or 15 *Barbus pentazona,* 6 *Acanthophthalmus kuhlii.* **South America:** 1 trio (1 male, 2 females) of Agassiz's dwarf cichlids or *Discrossus filamentosus,* 1 *Ancistrus,* 12 jewel tetras, 8 marbled hatchetfish. **Central Africa:** 1 trio of *Nanochromis transvestitus;* otherwise, like South America.

Clear, Plant-filled, Scarcely Moving Water

(See photograph, page 106.)

Biotope character: Lush plant growth with finely pinnate plants and water lilies on the sun-flooded edges of a flowing stream. Some current in the middle of the brook.

Aquarium arrangement: Abundant planting with plants of various growth forms on a 2^1/$_2$-in (6-cm)-thick substrate containing slow-release fertilizer. Open swimming area in foreground, in between driftwood caves. Slight current in open water.

Tank size: 47 × 20 × 20 in (120 × 50 × 50 cm); illumi-

What Do Fish Have to Do with Elephants?

Many elephants live in the African jungle. They come to drink and bathe at brooks and rivers. In the course of this, they trample on the soft, damp ground and leave footprints. Thus, small, clear pools develop. Some killifish can survive in these pools and even reproduce there. Unfortunately, there are no water fleas or other food animals in the minipools. But many insects fall in or lay their eggs there. So these fish still get some food. The fish live in such a minipool until it is again trampled by the next elephant. Then, the fish hop into the next pool.

Rocky biotope in Lake Malawi. All the fish species in the photograph are mbuna.

nate with two to three fluorescent tubes.

Suggestions for fish: **Australia:** 30 filament rainbow fish or 30 *Melanotaenia praecox*; 6 *Crossocheilus siamensis* for algae control. **Africa:** 1 pair of *Anomalochromis thomasi*, 6 upside-down catfish, 12 Congo tetras, 1 *Synodontis schoutedeni*; 1 pair of *Ancistrus* for algae control. **Asia:** 25 glass catfish; 6 sparkling panchax, 1 red-tailed black shark; 10 dwarf loaches. **South America:** 2 pairs of *Laetacara curviceps*, 10 *Otocinclus*; 8 diamond tetras, 12 penguin fish.

Rock Zone, Lake Malawi

(See photograph, page 110.)

Biotope character: Shallowly dropping off bank areas of the sun-flooded Lake Malawi with large algae-covered stones and rocks.

Aquarium arrangement: Arrange a rock pile of large stones topped on edge in the back two-thirds of the aquarium. Lay a thin Styrofoam layer first and the "ground stone" (see page 78). Place all stones so that the fish can swim through the rock wall. The substrate in front should be of fine gravel.

Tank size: 59 × 20 × 20 in (150 × 50 × 50 cm); illuminate with three fluorescent bulbs.

Suggestions for fish: 1 male and 5 females each of three Mbuna species (e.g., *Melanochromis* and *Pseudotropheus*).

It is important to keep at least a harem (one male and two females) of each species of Mbuna, to minimize agressive behavior.

How to Solve Maintenance Problems

Algae Problems in a Newly Established Aquarium

Situation: Some days after the aquarium is started up, there is vigorous algae growth (diatoms or filamentous algae).

Possible causes: The filter's biological filter effect is not working right because the filter bacteria necessary for it haven't yet developed sufficiently (see page 70). A further cause can be that the plants, though already planted, have not yet grown enough. Their metabolic activity is less as a result, and so they need scarcely any nutrients. Nutrients that you may have put into the aquarium as liquid plant fertilizer or fish food at such an early period in the aquarium's development are there for the algae to use for food without any competition.

Remedies: Apply several measures at the same time:

■ During the first few weeks, use activated carbon to filter, in addition.

■ Remove algae by hand or with an algae scraper.

■ Daily, change one-third of the aquarium water to remove the extra nutrients that are not yet needed or processed by plants and bacteria. Reduce the water changes when the algae problem abates.

■ Introduce some filter material from an already operating filter (friends, pet store) or some "filter starter" from the pet store into your filter. The bacteria contained in it will help jump-start your filter.

■ Install algae-eaters (see Algae Problems in an Already Established Aquarium, following).

■ Put in fast-growing stem or floating plants (hornwort, crystalwort, broad-leaved Indian fern), which compete with the algae for food. Don't use any chemical substances for combating the algae because they will disturb the development of the biological filter in progress.

Algae Problems in an Already-Established Aquarium

Situation: Strong growth of algae of only one or of various species.

Possible causes: In most cases, the nitrate content in the aquarium water is too high because of rare water changes, large fish population, or excess feeding. Sometimes an incorrect ratio among lighting, fertilizing, and water plant growth is to blame, for water plants should only be fertilized with the amount of nutrients that they can use. If you also fertilize and illuminate too much through inadequate maintenance, you are mainly fertilizing the undemanding algae.

Remedies: Undertake the following measures:

■ Do a daily partial water change for 1 week (one-third of the aquarium water).

■ Clean the filter and siphon the substrate with a hose.

■ Remove the algae as much as possible.

■ Don't fertilize the water plants as long as the algae problem exists.

■ For algae control, install one or two of the following animal species: *Crossocheilus siamensis*; otocinclus (*Otocinclus cf. affinis*); sucking loach (*Gyrinocheilus aymonieri*, see photograph page 113); bristle-mouth catfish (*Ancistrus dolichopterus*). The right species depends on the size of your aquarium (see

Can You Also Keep Frogs in an Aquarium?

Yes, for there are frogs that stay small and spend their entire lives in the water. One of these is called the dwarf platanna. You can buy African clawed frogs in many pet stores. If you want to keep one in your aquarium, you must observe the following:

Only small fish that will not harm the frog may live in your aquarium. Dwarf platannas are very useful, however. They often eat the tiresome small snails in your aquarium.

tables in the description section from page 14). A good filamentous algae-eater, available in your pet store as "grass shrimp" or "ghost shrimp," is the Japanese Garnele or Yamato-Numa-Ebi (*Caridina japonica*, see photograph, pages 102–103).

■ If the plants won't grow properly for you, read Aquariums Arranged Correctly and Beautifully (beginning on page 76).

Note: Don't use any chemicals to deal with algae because they don't correct the cause but can disturb the process of development of the biological filter.

Cloudy Water in Newly Established Tanks

Situation: Some hours to days after the tank is set up, the water suddenly turns milky looking.

It isn't the same cloudiness that is observable immediately after the water is added.

Possible causes: The cloudiness is produced by a harmless increase in numbers of certain bacteria.

Remedies: Don't do anything! The cloudiness is normal with certain types of water quality and will disappear after a few hours to days.

Sucking loaches (*Gyrinocheilus aymonieri*) are good algae-eaters for large tanks.

A beautiful
Malawi cichlid
(*Sciaenochromis freyeri*).

The Nitrate Concentration Won't Go Down

Situation: You have measured the nitrate concentration before and after the water change and determine only slight or no improvement. Usually, you also have algae problems in addition. In measuring the tap water, you discover nitrate concentrations that are distinctly more than 20 mg/L.

Possible causes: Your tap water already has a high nitrate content (see Nitrate Measurement and Removal, page 58).

Remedies: Provide your fish with nitrate-free (distilled) water from a reverse osmosis unit, an ion-exchanger desalinization system, or an ion-exchanger nitrate filter. The method that is most effective and appropriate for your tap water depends on the hardness of your local water supply and whether you also need to arrange to provide soft and salt-free water for your fish. Find out from your local pet store dealer about the most suitable method for you.

Snail Infestation

Situation: Small snails reproduce too much so that they are stuck all over the aquarium in great numbers.

Possible causes: They have entered your aquarium on water plants or live food. They have reproduced vigorously because they have particularly favorable conditions (much food with uneaten particles left there) and no enemies are present.

Remedies: Snails are not harmful except that they occasionally gnaw on water plants. You can try to inhibit the snail plague, but they can never be completely extermi-

nated. That is also not necessary. Do the following:

■ Feed the fish sparingly, but sufficiently, so that the snails find less food.

■ Siphon up food remnants left on the substrate.

■ Remove snails and their eggs by hand as often as possible.

■ Trap snails overnight in a snail trap: Put a saucer with a food tablet on it in the aquarium overnight. On top of it, put an overturned yogurt container that is poked full of small holes (snails pass through and fish don't). Next morning, there will be many snails in the saucer and they can be easily removed.

■ If it will work with the fish community you have in your aquarium, put in fish that like to eat small snails (*Anomalochromis thomasi*).

Puffers are of course specialized snail eaters, but only conditionally for community tanks. They nip the fins of fish that move slowly. Puffers should only be put with particularly nimble fish of the upper regions of the tank.

Note: Don't use any chemical anti-snail preparations, because they are also harmful to other useful inhabitants of the aquarium. In addition, too many dead snails considerably pollute the water.

Fish Become Too Large

Situation: Sometimes some fish species become considerably larger than you expected. You can no longer offer them appropriate living conditions.

Possible causes: You haven't gotten enough information before buying the fish. In addition, among the many responsible pet store dealers, there are some not so reputable who will sell you fish that will become too large for your aquarium.

The following list of fish that grow large may serve as a guideline; included are the final sizes that the fish can reach in the wild. None of these fish should be kept in an aquarium under 6 ft (2 m) long; some need materially more space. Even if some fish remain small in the aquarium, this does not indicate adaptation but maintenance that is incorrect!

Silver or Bala shark (Balantiocheilus melanopterus) (see photo, page 13), up to14 in (35 cm);

Chinese sailfin (Myxocyprinus asiaticus), up to about 24 in (60 cm); piranha (Pygocentrus nattereri), larger than 12 in (30 cm); shark catfish (Pangasius species) larger than 12 in (30 cm), some over 3 ft (1 m); red snakehead (Channa micropeltes), larger than 3 ft (1 m); arawana (Osteo-glossum bicirrhosum), up to 4 ft (1.2 m). Other large-growing fish species that are often offered are probably the African knife fish and "minisharks." They are only suitable for the freshwater aquarium as young fish, but later they need brackish water or saltwater, which you cannot offer them in a freshwater aquarium.

Remedies: Try to give the fish to an aquarist friend who has a bigger tank. If you were wrongly advised, take the fish back to the pet store dealer in order to have him pass them on to customers with suitable maintenance conditions. A reputable dealer will always take back one of his fish if there has been a misunderstanding. If you can find no one who can take care of the fish, you should get another, larger aquarium.

White Edge on Water Plant Leaves

Situation: A white, crusty deposit forms on the water plants. The pH can rise to values way above 8.

Causes: The water plants suffer from a deficiency of the important plant nutrient carbon dioxide. This condition occurs particularly often in aquarium waters with high carbonate hardness. The table on page 69 indicates that in carbonate-hard water there is little carbon dioxide available for the plants. To compensate for the deficiency of carbon dioxide, the plants take the carbon contained in the carbonate hardness agents. This causes lime deposits on the leaves, which are injurious to the plants, the carbonate hardness drops, and the pH value rises.

Remedies: Lower carbonate hardness through mixing with water low in carbonates and/or fertilize with carbon dioxide.

The Fish Don't Get Along with Each Other

Situation: Some fish harass others by chasing them through the tank, nipping their fins, not letting them get to food, or even eating them.

Possible causes: It is a matter of different species that are not suitable for a community tank because of their differing temperaments or sizes. If fish of one species bother those of another, your aquarium is too small for the territorial needs of the individual fish. With cichlid pairs, often the female and the male get into a "marital quarrel" unrelated to territorial needs, which may subside again after some time, but it doesn't always.

Remedies: Undertake the following measures:

■ Find out if you have made a mistake in composing your community (see profiles, from page 14). If yes, you should give away some of your fish or set up their own aquarium for them.

■ If you have too many territorial fish in too small an aquarium or a cichlid pair has had a falling out, increase the number of hiding places in your aquarium. In doing so, especially make use of the space below the surface of the water. Put caves there (e.g., plastic tubes hung on plastic-wrapped wire).

■ If the aggressive fish are still harassing the subordi-nate fish there, it's best to decrease the numbers of each species.

Water Change—and the Fish Are Suffering

Situation: After a water change, the fish are breathing hard, often stopping directly under the water surface. Measurement of pH gives values over 7.

Possible causes: Ammonia poisoning after a sudden jump of pH over 7: Ammonia is a poison that is created by the breakdown of biological products but normally is further converted by the filter bacteria into nitrate. At pH values under 7, if it is too long since the last water change, the tank is over-crowded, or too much biological waste has accumulated for other reasons and the bac-teria cannot completely process it, the relatively non-toxic ammonium ion is creat-ed as a by-product. If the pH of the water increases to over 7 because of a water change with alkaline water, the ammonium ion changes into poisonous ammonia.

Remedies: Do a careful 90 percent water change, in order to completely remove

Why Do Angelfish Have Stripes?

In the wild, angel-fish always live in places where uprooted forest trees are lying in the water. The many branches and twigs of these trees look like stripes under water. The striped marking of the angelfish resembles the branches of trees. From a dis-tance, the predatory fish only recognize the tangle of stripes. They cannot distin-guish between the branches and the angelfish. There-fore, we assume that the stripes of the angelfish serve to camouflage the fish.

the poisonous waste products from the aquarium. Clean the filter; siphon up the substrate. With sensitive fish that cannot tolerate a massive water change, you can also lower the pH with acidifying products from the pet store. But because these products only reconvert the ammonia into ammonium ion again, the cause is not remedied. Thus, an almost complete water change, but one that has been carefully spaced out over several days, is necessary nevertheless.

Vacation Substitutes

Situation: You want to take a vacation but have no one to take care of your fish.

Remedy: In an old, established aquarium that is not overpopulated, adult fish can tolerate a 2-week fasting period. Two weeks before you leave, check to be sure that all technical equipment is functioning perfectly (including the timer for the lighting). Thus, it is guaranteed that no technical complications will arise in your aquarium during your absense. A day before you

leave, change half the water in the aquarium. For longer absences, up to a month, you can use an automatic feeder. But then you should definitely find someone who can check regularly to see that none of the equipment has failed and can undertake a partial water change once (water prepared ahead of time in buckets). Give the caretaker your telephone number where you'll be vacationing or that of your pet store dealer, so that in case of doubt, a competent person can supply advice.

The angelfish
Pterophyllum altum needs soft, clean water.

My Aquarium

Here's space for your favorite picture.

Size and volume

Water type (see page 14)

Filter type and filter material

Lighting

Heater, other equipment

Set up date

Aquarium type (see page 106)

Aquarium fish and their attainable size

Types of food for the fish

Aquarium plants

Pet store dealer, name, address

Male filament or threadfin rainbow fish (*Iriatherina werneri*).

Fanwort (*Cabomba caroliniana*) needs very strong lighting.

Rivulus xiphidius.

USEFUL ADDRESSES AND LITERATURE

American Cichlid Association
c/o Howard Schmidt
P.O. Box 5351
Naperville, IL 60567-5351
(send SASE)

American Killifish Association
c/o Ronald Coleman
903 Merrifield Place
Mishawaka, IN 46544

Canadian Association of Aquarium Clubs
c/o Sarah Langhorne
95 East 31st Street
Hamilton, Ontario
Canada L8V 3N9

Aquarium Fish Magazine
P.O. Box 6050
Mission Viejo, CA 92690

Freshwater and Marine Aquarium
144 West Sierra Madre Boulevard
Sierra Madre, CA 91025

Internet Sources
http://www.petpath.com
Time, Inc.'s home page "You and Your Pet" and "Aqua-Life," a regular column on aquarium keeping. Additional resources for aquarium keepers can be found throughout the Web site.

Both Compuserve and America Online have special interest forums for aquarium keepers, available from libraries, bulletin boards, and chat groups.

Other Barron's Books
Hellner, Steffen, *Killifish*. Barron's Educational Series, Inc., Hauppauge, New York, 1990.

Scheurmann, Ines. *The New Aquarium Handbook*. Barron's Educational Series, Inc., Hauppauge, New York, 1986.

————. *Aquarium Plants Manual*. Barron's Educational Series, Inc., Hauppauge, New York, 1993.

Stadelmann, Peter. *Tropical Fish*. Barron's Educational Series, Inc., Hauppauge, New York, 1991.

Zurlo, Georg. *Cichlids*. Barron's Educational Series, Inc., Hauppauge, New York, 1991.

The Author
Ulrich Schliewen has been an enthusiastic aquarist since early childhood. He studied biology with a concentration in zoology at the University of Munich and has had close contact with the Max Planck Institute for Ethology and the Zoological State Collection in Munich. He has also traveled to South America, Central Africa, and Southeast Asia to study fish in their natural habitats. Mr. Schliewen is on the editorial board of *DCG-Info*, the publication of the German Cichlid Society, and has published articles in aquarists' magazines.

The Illustrator
Renate Holzner works as a freelance illustrator. Her broad repertoire extends from line drawings and photo-realistic illustration to computer graphics.

Acknowledgments
The author and the publisher of this book thank Eheim GmbH & Co. KG, Deizisau, for various internal and external filters and lighting information, Fohrmann Aquaristik GmbH, Lauenau, for the "Miniamazon" background and Schott-Glaswerke, Mainz, for the Siporax filter material.

Cover Photos and Chapter Openings

Front cover: Lace gourami (*Trichogaster leeri*) see large photo; fighting fish (*Betta splendens*) see small photo; pages 2–3: clown loaches (*Botia macracanthus*); pages 6–7: steel-blue killis (*Aphyosemion gardneri*); pages 56–57: rosy barbs (*Barbus conchonius*); pages 96–97: angelfish (*Pterophyllum scalare*); back cover: *Hypancistrus zebra*.

Photo Credits

Aqua Design Amano Co. Ltd./Takashi Amano: pages 62–63, 66–67, 80–81, 102–103; Büscher: pages 36 (fish); 38 top, 44 top, 104; Hartl: pages 22 bottom, 33, 37 top, 40 (fish), 42 bottom, 96–97, 100, 118; Hellner: page 48 center; Kahl: pages 2–3, 4–5 (plants), 9, 17 top, 19, 20 top, bottom, 21, 24 bottom (plants), 25, 26 bottom, 28 top, bottom, 29, 30 top, 36 (plants), 39 (plants), 40 (plants), 44 bottom (plants), 49 (plants) 50 top, bottom (plants), 51, 53 bottom, 54 center, 56–57, 64, 76–77, 107, 117 (plants), 121, 124 (plants); Kilian: pages 39, 117 (fish); Linke: pages 8, 26 top, 31 top, 32 top, bottom, 50 bottom (fish), 106, 108; Lucas: pages 13, 34 top, 37 bottom, 48 top, back cover; Lütje: 6–7, 124 (fish); Nieuwenhuizen: pages 4–5 (fish), 5 right, 11, 14, 15 top, 18 top, bottom, 23, 24 top, bottom (fish), 32 center, 34 bottom, 38 bottom, 49 (fish), 52 top, 59, 65, 73, 74, 91, 99, 101, 110, 113 top, 116, 126; Peither: pages 10, 17 top, 26 center, 30 bottom, 44 bottom (fish), 52 bottom, 68 left, right, 69, 78 top, bottom, 79 top, bottom, 87, 92–93, 123; Reinhard: page 53 top; Schliewen: pages 60, 109; Spreinat: pages 41, 46, top, bottom, 47, 90, 114; Staeck: pages 15 bottom, 31 bottom, 42 top, 45; Weidner: page 43; Werner: page 22 center; Wildekamp: pages 48 bottom, 54 top; Zurlo: cover, pages 22 top, 54 bottom, 113 bottom.

Synodontis schoutedeni.

Important Note

In this book, electrical equipment for maintenance of aquariums is described. Please be sure to read the manufacturer's safety precautions to prevent serious accidents.

Before buying a large tank, check how much weight the floor of your apartment can support in the location where you plan to set up your aquarium (see page 12). Sometimes water damage occurs as a result of broken glass, overflowing, or a leak in the tank. Thus, you should check insurance regulations and liability laws (see page 12).

Make sure that fish medications are out of reach of children. Avoid contact of the eyes, skin, and mucous membranes with caustic chemicals. In case of a contagious disease (such as fish tuberculosis), do not handle infected fish with bare hands or reach into the tank. The spines below the eyes of loaches and the fin spines of some catfish species can inflict wounds. Because these puncture wounds can trigger an allergic reaction, you should immediately see a physician if you get hurt.

First English language edition published in 1998 by Barron's Educational Series, Inc.

Published originally under the title *Aquarienfische Mein Heimtier*

Copyright © 1997 by Gräfe und Unzer verlag GmbH, Munchen
English translation © 1998 by Barron's Educational Series, Inc.

All inquiries should be addressed to:
Barron's Educational Series, Inc.
250 Wireless Boulevard
Hauppauge, New York 11788
http://www.barronseduc.com

Library of Congress Catalog No. 97-43423

International Standard Book No. 0-7641-5084-7

Library of Congress Cataloging-in-Publication Data
Schliewen, Ulrich.
    [Aquarienfische. English]
    Aquarium fish : how to care for them, feed them, and understand them / Ulrich Schliewen ; with photographs by expert aquarium photographers ; illustrations, Renate Holzner.
        p.   cm. — (Family pet)
    Includes bibliographical references (p. 125) and index.
    ISBN 0-7641-5084-7
    1. Aquarium fishes. 2. Aquariums. I. Title.
II. Series: Family pet series.
SF457.S33613   1998
639.34—dc21   97-43423
                                                      CIP

Printed in Hong Kong
9 8 7 6 5 4 3 2 1